I0796153

Colour in the Garden

Photography by Jason Ingram

Colour in the Garden
Stylish ideas for year-round colour

Lucy Bellamy

MITCHELL BEAZLEY

Contents

Introduction

'Consider the convenience of being able to put down a smear of colour just where you need it.'
Vita Sackville-West

I am hungry for colour. I want jam-red and acid-yellow, violet-blue and inchworm-green. I want cinnamon-orange with scorched yellow, liquorice and blackcurrant. I want amethyst, putty and smoky blue, the liminal in-between colours, and tart pink and purple that are rich and electric.

We all know instinctively that colour is good for us and it is colour that draws me out into my garden. Recent research shows that spending time outside fires up our synapses and recalibrates our senses, improving concentration, reducing stress and potentially boosting our immune systems. Breathing in phytoncides – the antimicrobial chemicals released by plants – and coming into contact with certain microbes found in soil is good for body and mind, with the potential to boost mood, reduce our heart rate and generally make us feel happier. You don't even need to be interested in plants to feel their benefits.

With most of us living in cities and urban areas, and the developers of new housing estates giving their properties increasingly tiny plots, every outdoor space, however small, has an important role to play in countering the climate crisis. A small urban garden, even a very small one made up completely of pots, is a living carbon sponge, taking carbon out of the atmosphere and locking it away. Additionally, plants provide food and shelter for pollinators and a wealth of other wildlife, increasing their numbers and contributing to local biodiversity. A medley of plants will also absorb rainfall after a deluge, preventing flash flooding, and provide cool air temperatures during hot weather, particularly in towns and cities.

When you add colour to a garden, it instantly creates atmosphere. While most of us know which colours we like and maybe even which colours we want in our garden, knowing the best plants to use to achieve this can be more difficult.

Here, then, is a deep dive into brilliant and life-changing colour: how to choose plants and how to use them creatively and inventively. Colour makes us feel alive; it is transporting and grounding. Even the smallest outdoor space has room for the joy of colour.

Tulipa 'Gavota' and *Rosa* × *odorata* 'Mutabilis' (tea rose)

As a consequence of the climate crisis, the way we use colour in the garden is changing – in favour of simpler flowers that benefit pollinators and are closer to the flowers found in nature.

A contemporary approach to colour

Modern colour

A vogue for simpler flowers that are less removed from those found in nature, paired with a more sustainable approach to our gardens, is changing the way we use colour outside. Gone are big, blowsy flowers, chosen like the colours on a paint chart. Plants with flowers like these, which have been bred to be as big as possible, need plenty of water and artificial plant foods and pesticides to sustain them. In the blowsiest flowers, the parts of the flower that are useful to pollinators – the nectaries, which contain the pollen and nectar – have been bred out completely to be replaced by extra petals. There is little room left for a pollinator to fit inside and limited or no pollen or nectar to forage. Such plants barely contribute to the biodiversity of a garden. With a low ratio of stem and leaf to flower on plants like these, once the flowers fade the whole plant needs to be replaced, stacking up its carbon footprint due to the fuel miles used for transporting it, the plastic needed for its pot and the industrial costs of its eventual recycling.

Tulipa 'Princess Irene', *T.* 'Queen of Night' and *T.* 'Estella Rijnveld'

Imagine instead a small outdoor space with layers of texture and colour, where plants of different heights and shapes merge and repeat, with colour coming through colour. A space where bright, painterly poppies pop, dahlias offer dollops of colour and, held on a scaffold of tall, narrow stems, the tiny flowers of verbena register together as they open to make a wash of colour. Where colourful buds give way to equally colourful flowers and later beautiful seedpods; where room around the plants is as important as the space they take up, so the light gets in, which, as it moves and plays, brings depth and even more colour.

Dahlia merckii (Merck dahlia)
Below: *Pulsatilla vulgaris* (pasque flower)

Tulipa 'Slawa' and *Lunaria annua* 'Chedlow Glow' (honesty)

Papaver somniferum 'Lauren's Grape' (opium poppy)

Succulents displayed in tiny pots on an impromptu table and in a giant urn. They include *Echeveria* 'Pink Champagne', × *Pachyveria* 'Opalina', *Aeonium* 'Pomegranate' and *Sedum sediforme* (ice plant).

Plan your space

'Sustainable urban gardens' contribution to combating climate change is so important that council or water tax cuts should be offered as incentives to anyone whose garden is more than 50% planted rather than covered by pavers or concrete.'
Professor Ross Cameron, University of Sheffield.

Adding colour to a garden instantly creates atmosphere, but it is the layout of the space – how you arrange it – that will define how you use it on a daily basis. Today, most of us want a hardworking, multifunctional outdoor area that is part living space, part workspace and part social space to enjoy with family and friends. Whether you are a hybrid worker with occasional days at home, want a place to eat supper outdoors or somewhere to spend time with your dog after work, thinking creatively about the layout of your garden is the essential starting point to every successful design. Try to bear the following points in mind:

- With many of us living in urban spaces and the developers of new estates giving properties only tiny plots, every garden has a vital role to play in countering the effects of climate change. Putting plants front and centre in the design of your outdoor space ranks high on the list of sustainable things you can do. Plants absorb pollution, including by locking in carbon, absorb rainwater runoff, mitigating the effects of flooding after a deluge of rain and protect the soil. They also offer food and shelter for pollinators and other wildlife.

- The plants that you choose and how you use them can be as much a part of the design of your garden as the paint colours, paving and pots. One way to highlight them is to create new borders that come right into the middle of the space. Freed from narrow beds and borders around the edges of the garden, the plants can become a dynamic kind of paint.

- Particularly in a small space, it is important to think about what you will see when you look out from the windows of your house and to give yourself something nice to look at. Well-placed plants, including in pots, are useful for concealing bins and recycling boxes. A beautifully filled container can mark the entrance to a bike store or the threshold between the house and the garden, so creating flow. Close to the walls, plants help to anchor a house in its location, especially in an urban setting.

Measuring less than 30 square metres (323 square feet), this small garden is packed with plants, creating a feeling of immersion – it is the plants rather than the hard landscaping that delineate the space. The warm pink tone of the brick wall aligns with the various pinks of plants such as *Allium sphaerocephalon* (drumstick allium), heightening the intensity of their colours.

The colours of walls or fences are integral to the look and feel of a small space. A nature-inspired hue on the walls here amplifies rather than competes with the colours of the plants. The textural, rendered finish also highlights the play of shadow and light beautifully.

Tall, textural plants with pops of colour, such as *Verbena bonariensis* (purple top), make the most of a long, narrow space alongside this modernist, open-plan home, connecting and enhancing both the house and the garden. From outside, the architecture of the building is amplified and from within, the plants draw attention out into the garden.

A stained wooden fence sets the scene in this shady garden. The dark backdrop merges with the shadowy gaps between the plants, meaning it is difficult to see where these end and the fence begins. This makes the small space seem bigger.

Elaeagnus 'Quicksilver' (oleaster) and the pinkish-white flowers of *Clematis montana* (Himalayan clematis) meld beautifully with this corrugated metal fence. Hung horizontally, its lines emphasize their pretty and painterly qualities.

Tulips, *Cynara cardunculus* (cardoon) and euphorbias pool into the middle of this space. The silver notes of the corrugated metal fence are picked up by the pale gravel path. Its ruddy notes are referenced in the dark tulip flowers.

Opposite: Red brick slips provide continuity between the interior and exterior spaces in this city garden. The plaster-pink render on the exterior walls is at once neutral and contemporary, enhancing the plant colours without taking over.

Dark brown Cor-Ten steel cladding offsets the pale colours of the plants in front. Its coppery hue and patina are reminiscent of the colours of tree bark and the dappled woodland light favoured by these shade-loving plants.

Contrasting with a timber floor and raised timber planters, small flowers ping out their colour, providing a vibrant accent while leaving plenty of room for the table and chairs.

Materials

The materials that you choose for the fixed elements in your garden, such as the floor and walls, provide a base colour against which your plants can work. What you use on the walls and the floor does more than create a level surface for a table or mark the extent of your garden's boundaries; these materials are also intrinsic to the look and feel of the space. In a small garden, it is best to limit the range of materials to a maximum of three and add accents in Cor-Ten steel, copper or canvas, for example, with the furniture and accessories.

- Use the garden's setting as a starting point and choose materials that will connect it to your locality. For example, referencing the urban landscape will anchor it in its surroundings and create a sense of place. From my own compact garden, I can see the corrugated steel of a garage roof, timber fencing, walls rendered in concrete, the silver of zinc guttering and pinky-toned brickwork, any of which could be successfully replicated in the material palette of the garden.

- If you are starting from scratch, use the best materials that your budget will allow, to futureproof your design. Different materials are available in an assortment of sizes, colours and textures, from gritty and textural concrete, to charred wood with depth and detail, to the uniformity of factory-made bricks and paving slabs, which have a geometric and architectural feel. Consider how the materials you choose will look in different weather conditions and how they will respond and change over time. Materials such as wood, slate or Cor-Ten steel improve with age, changing colour and developing a characterful patina.

A knapped flint wall offsets the dark brown of birch branches. Biscuit-coloured grout – a colour favoured by architects and interior designers – highlights the inherent irregularity of the flint.

- Take into account the whole garden, including its aspect (the direction your garden faces). Direct sun makes colours look more intense, while in shadow, paler-coloured materials are useful for bouncing light back into the garden. Changes in the direction of the light throughout the day can also be useful for drawing out the details of textural finishes.

- Spend time researching the different ways in which the same material can be used. Changing the pattern of, or spacing between, individual tiles, bricks or pavers is a good way to elevate humble materials into something really special.

- Consider the areas where paving, paths and boundaries meet. Will the materials you are using harmonize by replicating each other? A brick path laid in a staggered pattern that appears to fragment where it meets gravel will increase the sense of 'flow' around a small space.

- Transporting heavy materials can have an equally heavy carbon footprint. So, think locally and, where possible, try to exploit the existing materials on site in a creative way. If you are buying new paving, for example, take into account how it has been manufactured and even the eventual cost of its recycling.

- If you have a limited budget, use the best-quality materials in areas of your garden that you will see and use most often, and choose less expensive materials for the rest.

Soft plaster-pink wall render brings out the vibrant colour of *Papaver dubium* subsp. *lecoqii* 'Albiflorum' (Beth's poppy).

Choosing colour

Technically, the variety of colours available to use in a garden is infinite, but editing the palette down to a narrow band of colours allows you to experience them in way that using a lot of different colours does not. Since colour is experienced in the context of its surroundings, a limited palette allows you to pick up the connections between the colours you choose so that collectively, the plants will form a cohesive design.

Observation

It is easy to think of the colour of the plant as being the colour of its flowers. In most cases, this is the dominant colour and the one you notice first. But there is a difference between seeing a plant and looking at it properly and analyzing what you see. *Dianthus carthusianorum* (carthusian pink) has brilliant pink petals which, on closer examination, are marked with darker pink. The middle of the flower is white and the base of the flower (the calyx) and buds are brown-red. The stalks are chalky green with narrow, apple-green leaves.

Paying close attention to the details reveals a wide range of colours, any of which can be picked up and matched in other plants.

Close observation of *Dianthus carthusianorum* reveals a wide range of colours, including pink, dark pink, white, red and brown-red.

In this colourful combination, the dark calyx of *Dianthus carthusianorum* is picked up in the dark blotch at the base of *Papaver somniferum* 'Lauren's Grape' (opium poppy). The yellow centre of the poppy, rather than its petal colour, is echoed and repeated once more in the yellow flowers of *Verbascum bombyciferum* (mullein).

One way to develop a habit of observing plants more closely is to choose a favourite and list all the colours that you can see. Look at the colour of the petals and the buds, any petal markings and the reverse of the petals. Note the colour of the calyx and the middle of the flower, the style, stigma and stamens, the pollen, the stem colour, the colour of the leaves and any leaf markings. Any of these features are potential jumping-off points for creating a winning colour combination.

Next, build up your plant list by adding plants that share common colours. This might be in the colour of their petals or the centres of their flowers or their leaves or stems. Even if a plant includes just a small amount of a colour from the hero plant, it will still fit into the overall colour group.

Finally, add depth and dimension to the scheme by choosing plants in lighter and darker tones of the common colours. An easy way to do this is to imagine each colour as part of a sliding scale that you can run up and down, going from light to dark. The plants you include at this point will also have additional colours that you can pick up in more plants, to further broaden your scheme.

The rich, toffee-coloured flowers of *Verbascum* 'Petra' (mullein) are yellow at their edges and beautifully set off by the acid-yellow flowers of *Zizia aurea* (golden alexanders). The mahogany centres of the verbascum are picked up in the irises, as well as the crimson-red flowers of *Sanguisorba officinalis* 'Arnhem' (great burnet) growing elsewhere in the garden.

Metallic red, green and brown

Aspect Shade
Soil Any

This combination for shady conditions takes its cue from *Helleborus* × *hybridus* 'Slaty Blue' (hellebore), matching it with the small, stripy, olive-green and plum flowers of *Fritillaria acmopetala* (pointed-petal fritillary). The flower colours of these two plants are very similar tonally and both have an iridescent sheen. The dark midrib in the middle of the frond of the *Dryopteris wallichiana* (alpine wood fern) and, to a lesser degree, in the *Asplenium scolopendrium* Undulatum Group (hart's tongue fern) reference their red-brown colour, while their fresh, bright leaf blades contribute to the myriad greens. *Helleborus foetidus* (stinking hellebore) has virescent green flowers that add a sharp note, offsetting the other colours and opening up the planting scheme.

Dryopteris wallichiana
(alpine wood fern)

Helleborus × hybridus 'Slaty Blue' (hellebore)

Asplenium scolopendrium Undulatum Group (hart's tongue fern)

Thalictrum 'Anne' (meadow rue)

Helleborus foetidus (stinking hellebore)

Fritillaria acmopetala (pointed-petal fritillary)

Thalictrum 'Elin' (meadow rue)

Crimson, blackcurrant and pink

Aspect Sun
Soil Any

Darker and lighter hues of blackcurrant, crimson and pink, in varying amounts, make up this pretty palette. Early in spring, *Fritillaria meleagris* (snake's head fritillary) has plum and white chequerboard flowers. Big dollops of colour from the opium poppy *Papaver somniferum* 'Lauren's Grape' (opium poppy) reference its red tones in summer, which are picked up and repeated by the bursts of colour from *Sanguisorba officinalis* 'Arnhem' (great burnet). *Linaria purpurea* 'Canon Went' (purple toadflax) has tiny, snapdragon-like flowers. Pale pink, they open incrementally and register lightly to create a haze of smudgy colour. *Rosa × odorata* 'Mutabilis', a tea rose, has crimson shoots and red and apricot flowers.

Papaver somniferum
'Lauren's Grape'
(opium poppy)

Fritillaria meleagris
(snake's head fritillary)

Linaria purpurea 'Canon Went'
(purple toadflax)

Tulipa 'Ballade'
(tulip)

Sanguisorba officinalis 'Arnhem'
(great burnet)

Rosa × *odorata* 'Mutabilis'
(tea rose)

Salvia officinalis 'Purpurascens'
(purple sage)

Marmalade, bitter orange and yellow

Aspect Sun
Soil Any

Bitter orange, tangerine and marmalade look wonderful together, enlivened in this planting scheme with flits of white and yellow. *Narcissus poeticus* var. *recurvus* (old pheasant's eye) is the first in a procession of flowers with orange tints. *Tulipa* 'Artist' is next, appearing among the foliage of the later-flowering perennials; the flash of green on its petals highlights their varying shades of green. *Helenium* 'Moerheim Beauty' (sneezeweed) and the aster *Symphyotrichum* 'Oktoberlicht' (aster) have mustard and canary-yellow centres, adding tonal variation. Note also the mahogany centres of the marigold and geum flowers, which add depth as well as an extra layer of colour.

Narcissus poeticus var. *recurvus* (old pheasant's eye)

Tulipa 'Artist'
(tulip)

Geum 'Prinses Juliana'
(avens)

Verbascum 'Petra'
(mullein)

Calendula officinalis 'Zeolights'
(pot marigold)

Symphyotrichum 'Oktoberlicht'
(aster)

Helenium 'Moerheim Beauty'
(sneezeweed)

Cool blue, lilac and yellow

Aspect Sun
Soil Well drained

This cool lilac, yellow and blue palette takes its cue from the colours of *Gladiolus papilio* (butterfly sword lily), using plants in inky and electric blue, soft yellow and violet. *Allium* 'Millennium' (ornamental onion) and *Salvia* 'Nachtvlinder' (sage) are lighter and darker versions of the colour of its petals, while the brilliant yellow *Tulipa sylvestris* (wild tulip) picks up on the yellow markings at its tips. *Cerinthe major* 'Purpurascens' (honeywort) has a graduated colour change, moving from blue to green, which pulls the vibrant *Muscari aucheri* 'Ocean Magic' (grape hyacinth) into the scheme.

Tulipa sylvestris (wild tulip)

Gladiolus papilio
(butterfly sword lily)

Allium 'Millennium'
(ornamental onion)

Melica altissima 'Alba'
(Siberian melic)

Cerinthe major 'Purpurascens'
(honeywort)

Salvia 'Nachtvlinder'
(sage)

Muscari aucheri 'Ocean Magic'
(grape hyacinth)

Violet, yellow and white

Aspect Partial shade
Soil Any

Pale colours are useful for throwing light into shady spots, and this palette uses plants that all thrive in partial shade. The Sicilian honey garlic, *Allium siculum* (formerly in the *Nectaroscordum* genus), is a pendulous type of allium with pink and green, stripy flowers. It makes a good match for the green-flashed petals of *Tulipa* 'Spring Green' and is energized by the bright violet flowers of *Lunaria annua* 'Corfu Blue' (honesty). *Geum* 'Lemon Drops' (avens) picks up the creamy yellow of the tulip petals. Deep purple *Allium hollandicum* 'Purple Sensation' (Dutch garlic) adds a dark, rich element, offsetting the other colours while remaining true to the palette.

Tulipa 'Spring Green' (tulip)

Allium siculum
(Sicilian honey garlic)

Allium hollandicum 'Purple Sensation' (Dutch garlic)

Luzula nivea
(snowy wood-rush)

Geum 'Lemon Drops'
(avens)

Lunaria annua 'Corfu Blue'
(honesty)

Astrantia major subsp. *involucrata* 'Shaggy' (masterwort)

Mulberry, silver and pink

Aspect Sun
Soil Well drained

This combination draws on the colours of *Allium tripedale* (ornamental onion), a telescopically tall allium, using the dark and light pinks of its stripes. *Astrantia major* 'Florence' (masterwort) shares a common colour with its pink flowers, while *Nepeta* 'Six Hills Giant' (catmint) and *Dierama robustum* (wandflower) pick up on its silvery-grey hue. The bold, but narrowly drawn, starburst flowers of *Allium stipitatum* 'Mount Everest' (ornamental onion) repeat the white markings at the tips of its blooms, which also reappear in the tiny flowers of *Briza media* (common quaking grass).

Tulipa 'Ronaldo' has a plum flower and a white bloom to its petals, and so sits easily within this light-reflecting palette.

Dierama robustum (wandflower)

Astrantia major 'Florence'
(masterwort)

Allium tripedale
(ornamental onion)

Tulipa 'Ronaldo'
(tulip)

Nepeta 'Six Hills Giant'
(catmint)

Allium stipitatum 'Mount Everest'
(ornamental onion)

Briza media
(common quaking grass)

Yellow, pink and blue

Aspect Sun
Soil Well drained

Different colours of the same hue are key to this yellow, pink and violet-blue scheme, which uses *Papaver dubium* subsp. *lecoqii* 'Albiflorum' (Beth's poppy) as a point of reference. This poppy's luminous pink petals, each with a white blotch near the base, its near-black anthers and lime and yellow centre are matched by the violet flowers of *Salvia sclarea* (clary), the small, silvery white blooms of *Ammi majus* (false bishop's weed) and the green and yellow flowers of *Euphorbia oblongata* (Balkan spurge). *Salvia sclarea* has grey leaves – indicative of its affinity with sunny spots - which ping back light, seemingly repeating the translucency of the poppy's paper-thin flowers.

Euphorbia oblongata
(Balkan spurge)

Ammi majus
(false bishop's weed)

Salvia sclarea
(clary)

Papaver dubium subsp.
lecoqii 'Albiflorum'
(Beth's poppy)

Liquorice, pink and blue

Aspect Sun
Soil Any

This textural combination emphasizes small flowers and repeating patterns. Salvias, nepetas and verbenas all have transparent qualities, which means the colours of their flowers register against themselves as well as each other. *Verbena officinalis* 'Bampton' (vervain) is one of my favourite plants for a small outdoor space, as it is as useful for its dark liquorice-coloured stems and tiny, dark leaves as for its true pink flowers. In this planting scheme it does double-duty, echoing the near-black stems of *Salvia nemorosa* 'Caradonna' (Balkan clary) as well as the pink flowers of *S.* 'Dyson's Joy' (sage).

Salvia 'Dyson's Joy' (sage)

Salvia nemorosa 'Caradonna'
(Balkan clary)

Verbena officinalis 'Bampton'
(vervain)

Nepeta racemosa 'Walker's Low'
(catmint)

Agapanthus 'Black Magic'
(African lily)

Symphyotrichum 'Little Carlow'
(aster)

Lavandula angustifolia 'Hidcote'
(English lavender)

Choosing plants

As you decide which plants you'd like to include in your outdoor space, it is vital to take the environmental conditions – known as the microclimate – of your garden into account. By selecting plants that are naturally suited to this microclimate, be it sun or shade, and to its soil type, you will create a garden where everything grows with ease. The late British gardener Beth Chatto famously coined the phrase 'right plant, right place' to decribed the importance of matching a plant to its favoured conditions, informed by the habitat in which it grows in the wild. Respecting the innate preferences of each plant in your garden creates a space that needs less intervention from you and that is more enjoyable to maintain.

Since plants that benefit from the same conditions often share common physical characteristics, this also means that, from a design perspective, the palette of plants you choose will sit comfortably together and feel instinctively right.

Verbascum 'Petra' (mullein) and *Geum* 'Alabama Slammer' (avens)

Soil

Understanding your soil is key to choosing the most suitable plants, ensuring they thrive and benefit from the available resources. Soil is made of sand, silt and clay in varying amounts, as well as organic matter like rotting leaves, soil-dwelling insects and microorganisms, air and water.

A 'sandy' soil drains easily, as it doesn't hold on to water. It can be prone to drying out, although plants will never sit in wet conditions. It is lightweight and easy to work but also hungry due to the limited nutrients. A 'clay' soil holds on to water and is high in nutrients. It is heavy and difficult to dig, sticky in winter and baked hard and dry in summer. A 'loam' soil is a balanced blend of the two, being easy to work and relatively nutritious.

To identify your soil, take a handful, lightly squeeze and then release it, keeping it in your hand. If it holds its shape, it is a clay soil. If it crumbles immediately, it is a sandy soil and if it holds its shape but falls apart after a gentle nudging, it is loam.

Plants with scant, narrow foliage, such as *Tulbaghia violacea* (society garlic), usually thrive in soils that don't hold on to water, while foliage that is silver in appearance hints at a plant that prefers sun.

Aspect

The aspect of your garden – whether it faces north, south, east or west when viewed from the house – will determine how much sun or shade it gets. The amount of sun or shade, and where this falls throughout the day, changes across the days and months and also through the year. Knowing the aspect of your outdoor space will help you understand how to use it and what to plant where. In the Northern Hemisphere, a south-facing garden is the most sunny, as the sun goes directly over it as it moves from east to west. A north-facing garden is mostly in shadow, as the sun is obstructed by the house. A garden with an easterly aspect is sunny in the morning and shady in the afternoon and into the evening, while a west-facing garden is in shadow in the morning, but sunny in the afternoon and into the evening in summer. If your garden gets more than six hours of sun a day, it is considered sunny, even if it doesn't get that much sun in winter. These aspects are reversed if you live in the Southern Hemisphere.

Other factors that can affect the amount of sun in your garden include adjacent buildings, which create dense, heavy shade, and overhanging trees, which create intermittent, or dappled, light.

As well as ensuring they thrive, limiting your choice of plants to those suited to the soil and aspect of your garden inevitably results in a palette that looks and feels right. Plants that benefit from the same conditions share similiar physical features, which will complement each other. Typically, for example, plants that like sun have small or narrow leaves to reduce the amount of water lost through transpiration and are often silvery in appearance to throw off the heat, whereas plants that thrive in shade have large or broad leaves in order to catch as much of the available sunlight as possible.

Layers

In nature, plants arrange themselves effortlessly into layers. The shoots of *Galanthus* (snowdrop) are hardened at their tips to push through the frozen ground to flower early in the window of light before the tree canopy above them comes into leaf. Similarly, *Primula* (primrose) love and proliferate in the broken light and shade under deciduous trees. In a meadow during summer, *Leucantheumum vulgare* (ox-eye daisy) and buttercups hover above low-growing grasses and beneath *Anthriscus sylvestris* (cow parsley), all of the plants bidding to be the first to catch the attention of pollinators flying past.

The way in which plants are arranged similarly makes a big difference in a garden. Using a combination of taller and shorter plants creates texture and filters the light - the essential ingredient for transforming a simple colour palette into an array of hues. A variety of plants also increases biodiversity.

The physical characteristics of some types of plants mean that they lend themselves well to being used in this way.

The architectural, pinky-green flowers of *Allium siculum* hover above violet-flowered *Salvia nemorosa* 'Caradonna' (Balkan clary).

Plants with flowers that appear to hover

Plants such as *Orlaya grandiflora* (white laceflower), *Allium siculum* (Sicilian honey garlic) and *Tulbaghia violacea* (society garlic) have narrow, usually straight, stems that are almost invisible in comparison to their flowers, so these appear to hover, as if suspended in mid-air. Plants like these are best used in number and arranged in a repeating pattern, letting you play with the spaces between them.

Tulbaghia violacea (society garlic)

With narrow stems and scant foliage, the white umbels of *Orlaya grandiflora* appear to float, and in a small garden the eye skips from one flower to the next.

The tiny flowers of *Verbena bonariensis* (purple top), *Linaria purpurea* 'Canon Went' (purple toadflax) and *Verbena officinalis* 'Bampton' (vervain).

Plants with tiny flowers

Diaphanous plants, such as *Linaria purpurea* 'Canon Went' (purple toadflax), *Verbena officinalis* 'Bampton' (vervain) and *Sanguisorba officinalis* 'Arnhem' (great burnet), are made up of hundreds of tiny flowers that open at the same time and register together to make a haze of colour. The small scale and wide distribution of their flowers means that the plants retain a degree of transparency, letting you see a little of what is growing beyond them. Although the flowers are tiny as individuals, they register strongly in number and the mist of colour this creates provides a useful foil through which to view contrasting colours.

Ground-hugging plants

While some plants are tall and airy in habit, others are low and dense, and the empty space above the ground-huggers is as useful as the physical space that they take up. They provide a helpful understorey for taller plants, highlighting their loftiness and giving them the space they need to catch the light. In addition, low-growing plants act like a mulch, covering the soil and shading it, thus reducing the drying effects of the sun and wind. This keeps the amount of additional water a garden needs to a minimum.

Ground-hugging *Salvia rosmarinus* (rosemary) is an enduring green presence in any garden. Its narrow foliage makes patterns of its own.

Plants with single and double flowers

A 'double' flower is one that has been bred to have two or more rows of petals in comparison to a 'single' flower, which has just one row. Single flowers have a graphic outline that is more legible in a small space and their petals also catch the light more easily.

The extra petals in a double flower come from the development of the flower's stamens into secondary petaloids, which resemble flower petals, and as a consequence are without – or in some cases almost without – pollen and nectar. There is also little room for a pollinator to get inside the flower.

Single flowers are more easily seen by both people and pollinators. Here, a single row of petals catches the light, highlighting the colours of *Dahlia* 'Bishop of Auckland'.

In this scheme the colour of *Verbascum phoeniceum* 'Violetta' (purple mullein) echoes that of *Allium* 'Millennium' (ornamental onion) but in a lighter hue, while the vibrant orange flowers of *Geum* 'Totally Tangerine' (avens) are picked up in the yellow foliage and stems of the *Deschampsia* grass. The small flowers of this grass have a pinkish tone, which is also present in the allium's flowers.

Seasonal change

Seasonal change is a good thing – research shows that attachment to our gardens is much stronger when we are aware of how they shift and alter day to day. Noticing this can often involve looking closely and tuning into the smaller details.

Choose plants that flower at different times

Some plants flower early, taking advantage of the light and soil moisture in spring to get ahead of the competition. Bulbs such as tulips are brilliant at this. Other plants spend most of the summer building up their resources underground to flower late in the season with a vibrant flicker of colour. Mixing and matching plants that flower at different times of year is an excellent way to ensure a continuous cycle of colour.

6 early flowerers

Lunaria annua 'Corfu Blue'	1
Salvia rosmarinus	
Thymus 'Fragrantissimus'	
Tulipa 'Artist'	
Tulipa sylvestris	2

1 2

7 late flowerers

Anemone Wild Swan ('Macane001')	1
Dahlia merckii	2
Dierama pulcherrimum	3
Salvia patens	4
Sanguisorba tenuifolia var. *alba*	
Symphyotrichum 'Little Carlow'	5

1

2

3

4

5

Choose plants that straddle the seasons

Use plants that flower for more than one season alongside more transient blooms. The colour-changing tea rose, *Rosa* × *odorata* 'Mutabilis', is super long-flowering, starting in late spring and continuing late into autumn. Other plants like *Papaver* (poppy) are more fleeting – and all the more valuable for it.

Rosa × *odorata* 'Mutabilis' **1**

Papaver dubium subsp. *lecoqii* 'Albiflorum' **2**

1

2

Look for colour shifters

Choose plants that change mercurially throughout their annual cycle, contributing a different colour as they transition from bud to flower or from flower to seedpod. Some plants are as colourful in bud or seedhead as they are in full flower, shifting colour as they move through their cycle. *Pulsatilla vulgaris* (pasque flower), for example, has purple flowers with yellow centres in spring that evolve to vanilla seedheads in summer.

6 colourful seedpods

Eschscholzia californica 'Ivory Castle'	
Eryngium eburneum	2
Papaver somniferum	
Pulsatilla vulgaris	1
Symphyotrichum 'Little Carlow'	3
Thalictrum delavayi	4

1

3

4

2

Salvia 'Dyson's Joy' (sage) and *S. nemorosa* 'Amethyst' (Balkan clary) are both well matched by the pink flowers of *Papaver dubium* subsp. *lecoqii* 'Albiflorum' (Beth's poppy). The poppy's seedpods have an iridescent sheen that catches the light, drawing attention to the white petal markings of the sage.

Using clever plant choices in creative combinations, here are seven small gardens to inspire.

Seven small spaces

Painterly palette [1]

Aspect Sun
Soil Well drained

The garden at The Exchange (a community-owned space), by designer Sarah Price and head gardener Colin Stewart, pivots around crimson, silver and pink. Corrugated iron fencing draws on the garden's urban setting and provides a flattering backdrop for a painterly combination of plants. The metallic tones of silver-leaved *Elaeagnus* 'Quicksilver' (oleaster) and *Cynara cardunculus* (cardoon) throw light around the space and offer a subtle contrast among brighter, zestier greens. Their colours highlight a richly hued and intentionally limited palette of flowers in tonally aligned colours. *Rosa × odorata* 'Mutabilis' (tea rose) has crimson-bronze shoots in spring that open to apricot flowers; these deepen to crimson as they age. It makes a good match for two-toned *Tulipa* 'Slawa' and stripy *T.* 'Spring Green', which both contribute a bright note, lifting the scheme and making the other colours in the garden appear livelier than they might without them. Freed from narrow beds and borders, the patterns of the plants mimic those they make in nature, while bringing them into the middle of the space highlights their colours.

Earthy-coloured brickwork laid in a herringbone pattern, used for the path, and a copper-hued table add extra layers of colour that complement rather than compete with the colours of the plants. Pooling into the middle of the space, it is their colours that are front and centre.

Featured plants

Clematis montana ★ **Himalayan clematis**

Cynara cardunculus ★ **cardoon**

Dryopteris erythrosora ★ **copper shield fern**

Elaeagnus 'Quicksilver' ★ **oleaster**

Euphorbia ★ **spurge**

Lunaria annua 'Chedlow Glow' ★ **honesty**

Pinus halepensis ★ **Aleppo pine**

Rosa × odorata 'Mutabilis' ★ **tea rose**

Tulipa 'Slawa' ★ **tulip**

Tulipa 'Spring Green' ★ **tulip**

• A double act of well-chosen plants and carefully considered materials from within the same narrow tonal band creates a cohesive space, with colour extending right up to the boundaries of the garden.

• Spring-flowering bulbs are useful for exaggerating the seasons. Easy to grow from bulbs, tulips are planted in autumn and are available in a vast array of colours.

• Different plants are used in various spots, according to the microclimate. In sun, *Lunaria annua* 'Chedlow Glow' (honesty) and tulips jostle with silver-leaved cardoons. At the foot of a wall, ferns and inky-foliaged *Viola labradorica* (Labrador violet) make dry shade their own.

• Brickwork for paths is laid in a herringbone pattern, replicating the floor inside the building and creating an easy flow between the two spaces.

• Pots in different sizes and shapes repeat the garden's colours. Bigger pots need watering less often than smaller ones and are easier to maintain.

Opposite: In the shadow of steps, rust-tinged ferns and the silvery cones of *Pinus halepensis* (Aleppo pine) play on the rusty tone of the railing and a grey breeze-block (cinder block) wall.

Sunlight filters softly through the tallest plants – here, *Eleagnus* 'Quicksilver' – dropping through to the lower layers.

The emergent fronds of *Dryopteris erythrosora* (copper field fern) repeat the colours found elsewhere.

The plants used in the open garden repeat in pots, seamlessly connecting the two. Two-tone *Lunaria annua* 'Chedlow Glow' continues the bicoloured theme of the tulips and has the added benefit of silver seedpods in autumn.

Geometric brickwork seems to fragment where it meets the plants, enhancing the free-flowing design.

Colour-changing *Rosa* × *odorata* 'Mutabilis' chimes with the colours of other plants used in the space.

Two-tone *Tulipa* 'Slawa' (above) and *T.* 'Spring Green' (right) are reliably perennial, returning to flowering every spring.

The giant, jagged, silver leaves of *Cynara cardunculus* bring levity to the darker greens.

The patina of the iron fence throws silver-pink *Clematis montana* and *Elaeagnus* 'Quicksilver' into relief.

Featured plants

Betula 'Fascination' ★ **birch**

Erysimum 'Bowles's Mauve' ★ **perennial wallflower**

Geranium Rozanne ('Gerwat') ★ **cranesbill**

Nepeta 'Six Hills Giant' ★ **catmint**

Pennisetum alopecuroides 'Hameln' ★ **Chinese fountain grass**

Poa labillardierei ★ **New Zealand blue grass**

Salvia × *sylvestris* 'Mainacht' ★ **wood sage**

All the blues [2]

Aspect Sun
Soil Loam

Smoky blue, lilac and pink are at the heart of this design by Mirira Harris in a small city garden. Blue-flowered *Nepeta* 'Six Hills Giant' (catmint), violet *Salvia* × *sylvestris* 'Mainacht' (wood sage), the purple cranesbill *Geranium* Rozanne ('Gerwat') and a pinky-violet perennial wallflower, *Erysimum* 'Bowles's Mauve', create a tessellating understorey beneath a series of small trees, which are suited to the scale of the space. The birch tree, *Betula* 'Fascination', displays characterful change throughout the seasons and its branching stems strike an informal note that feels in keeping with the design of the garden.

The impact of the *Poa labillardierei* (New Zealand blue grass) belies the size of the space it takes up. Its hovering flowers are quasi-transparent and pick up on the gleaming white tones of the peeling bark of the birch tree, and the two work beautifully together to lift the blues of the scheme.

A stepped, wooden floor turns this small space into a garden of many parts, with different areas in sun or shade.

From within the house, a square window frames the view of the garden and looks out onto a colourful and leafy scene, drawing the eye outwards and providing a constant reminder of the vibrant garden beyond.

Erysimum 'Bowles's Mauve' (perennial wallflower)

Nepeta 'Six Hills Giant' (catmint)

- Designer Miria Harris brings plants right up to the walls of the house, fostering a sense of seclusion and a feeling of immersion in nature.

- With its delicate canopy, a birch tree gently filters the light and casts dappled shadows, as well as muffling the city's noise and sheltering the garden from the hustle and bustle of the street outside.

- A thoughtful combination of tall and short plants creates interesting layers, drawing the eye deeper into the garden and away from the buildings beyond.

- A staggered pathway reveals the garden gradually, making it appear bigger than it otherwise might.

Betula 'Fascination' has an airy canopy, allowing plants to grow happily beneath.

The colours in the garden are heightened by the colour of the house walls, which pick up on the pinky tones in the plants.

Opposite: From inside the house, the view of the garden is a vignette of colour, packed with plants such as *Pennisetum alopecuroides* 'Hameln' (Chinese fountain grass) and *Nepeta* 'Six Hills Giant'.

Balance of colours [3]

Aspect Sun
Soil Loam

A medley of plants with colours on a sliding scale of pinks, reds and purples, offset by acid-green and yellow, are integral to this small city garden designed by Matt Evans. Divided by two parallel paths on either side of a block of plants, this airy palette is a beautiful combination. Darker tones of pink, violet and brown in the flowers of *Salvia* 'Nachtvlinder' (sage), *Digitalis parviflora* (small-flowered foxglove) and *Fuchsia magellanica* (hardy fuchsia) add depth and provide a backdrop for the brighter colours. The silver tones in the leaves and stems of *Verbascum bombyciferum* 'Polarsommer' (mullein) and coppery-bronze foxglove flowers lend a metallic note that adds an extra dimension. A corrugated fence, hung vertically and painted pale green, delineates a space for an eclectic mix of pots and planters, setting them apart as something special while cleverly integrating them into the scheme.

Featured plants

Astrantia major subsp. *involucrata* 'Shaggy' ★ **masterwort**

Digitalis parviflora ★ **small-flowered foxglove**

Euphorbia seguieriana subsp. *niciciana* ★ **spurge**

Fuchsia magellanica ★ **hardy fuchsia**

Hakonechloa macra ★ **Japanese forest grass**

Salvia 'Nachtvlinder' ★ **sage**

Thalictrum 'Anne' ★ **meadow rue**

Verbascum bombyciferum 'Polarsommer' ★ **mullein**

The dark, inky stems of *Thalictrum* 'Anne' pick up on the darker notes of *Salvia* 'Nachvlinder'.

Together with *Fuchsia magellanica* and *Digitalis parviflora* they create pools of deeper colour.

Fuchsia magellanica flowers and *Digitalis parviflora* seedheads

• Plants of different heights are packed together, filling all the available space and leaving no bare soil between them. Being in the garden is an immersive experience – wherever you are, you are surrounded by plants.

• Garden designers tend to use fewer plants in greater numbers, with the same plants repeating, so the eye skips among them.

• The dark colours in the scheme take their cue from the tones of *Fuchsia magellanica* and repeat in varying intensities. The violet flowers of *Salvia* 'Nachtvlinder' pick up on its purple corolla, while the pink flowers of *Linaria purpurea* 'Canon Went' (purple toadflax) and pinkish-brown blooms of *Digitalis parviflora* echo its pink petal colour. Electric-green *Euphorbia seguieriana* subsp. *niciciana* (spurge) and vibrant green *Hakonechloa macra* (Japanese forest grass) provide a contrast, energizing the scheme.

• The materials have been chosen with the same skill and consideration as the plants. Concrete, metal and brick-red clay pots take into account the garden's urban setting.

• The folding table and chairs, chosen for practical purposes, are pale grey, echoing the colour of the aged wooden fence and deck and accentuating the colours of the plants.

Opposite: Steely, green-white *Astrantia major* subsp. *involucrata* 'Shaggy' (masterwort) is a super long-flowering perennial and adds a further metallic note to the scheme.

Linaria purpurea 'Canon Went' (purple toadflax)

Fuchsia magellanica (hardy fuchsia)

Towering above an understorey of perennials and grasses, the height and empty space around the *Verbascum bombyciferum* 'Polarsommer' mean it can take advantage of the levels and direction of the natural light.

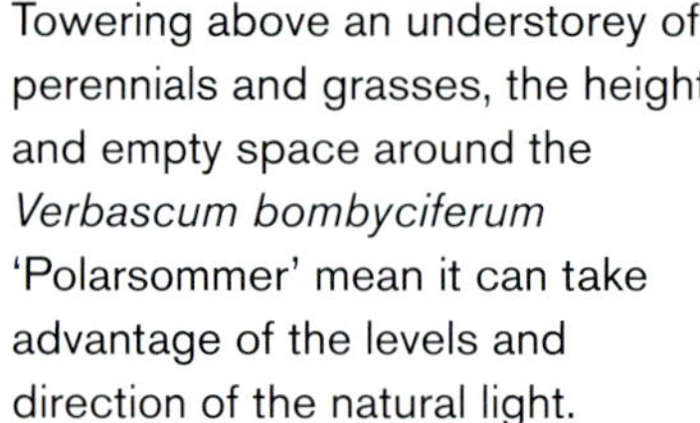

Euphorbia seguieriana subsp. *niciciana* (spurge)

Hakonechloa macra (Japanese forest grass)

Liminal colours [4]

Aspect Sun
Soil Well drained

A masterclass in offbeat colour, this garden by designer Sarah Price uses plants of different weights, heights and hefts to build up layers of colour. Set among a combination of bright, glaucous and grey-greens – colours that mix easily with almost every other colour – the palette takes its cue from the creamy lemon, vanilla and plum flowers of *Iris* 'Benton Olive', which are picked up in the rich violet flowers of *Linaria maroccana* 'Licilia Violet' (Moroccan toadflax), the purple stems of *Angelica archangelica*, the ruby-red foliage of *Atriplex hortensis* var. *rubra* (red orach) and the creamy yellow blooms of *Iris* ' Benton Susan'.

Pots and containers in varying sizes and shapes mimic the colours and textures found throughout the garden, including on the floor and the walls and in the colours of the plants.

Crushed bricks, a waste material left over from the construction of the space, are used as a mulch to cover the soil next to the path and between the plants. Perfectly matched to the colour of the pavers, this feels intentionally modern.

Painted in soft pink and ochre, the colours on the walls extend the scheme right up to and onto the boundaries, which counterbalances the more complex colours of the plants. Brought into the middle of the garden, the plants are highlighted and benefit from the play of light.

Featured plants

Angelica archangelica ★ **angelica**

Atriplex hortensis var. *rubra* ★ **red orach**

Briza media ★ **common quaking grass**

Cenolophium denudatum ★ **Baltic parsley**

Crassothonna capensis ★ **little pickles**

Elaeagnus 'Quicksilver' ★ **oleaster**

Eschscholzia californica 'Ivory Castle' ★ **California poppy**

Iris 'Benton Olive' ★ **iris**

Iris 'Benton Susan' ★ **Iris**

Lathyrus odoratus 'Matucana' ★ **sweet pea**

Linaria maroccana 'Licilia Violet' ★ **Moroccan toadflax**

Tulbaghia violacea ★ **society garlic**

- Using a pared-back palette of yellows and violets in darker and lighter hues imbues this space with atmosphere.

- Large-scale containers offer plenty of scope for creating exciting plant combinations. Repeating the colours found elsewhere in the garden in the plants they contain feels fresh and purposeful.

- A roughly hewn, rectangular wooden table has a suitably organic feel. The dark brown wood stain used on its legs and those of the bench riff on the dark brown bark of a tree as well as adding tonal variation.

- An impromtu plant stand made from a pile of leftover bricks highlights a large, rough-hewn bowl of *Sedum pulchellum* (flowering moss) and *Tulbaghia* 'Purple Eye' (society garlic), lifting it up to eye level to better appreciate the contents. The plant *Tulbaghia* appears elsewhere in the garden: *T. violacea* is growing in the soil at the foot of the plant stand. The roughly cast texture of the bowl offers shelter for wildlife.

Lathyrus odoratus 'Matucana' (below) is a two-toned sweet pea in amethyst and violet, which chimes beautifully with the wider palette. It softens the plant stand supporting the rough-hewn bowl (above).

Brown glazed pots with pink and green succulents, including *Curio talinoides* subsp. *mandraliscae* and *Crassothonna capensis* (little pickles), draw attention to the dark struts of the table.

On narrow stems, umbels of pale pink *Tulbaghia violacea* appear to hover above the violet-blue, snapdragon-like flowers of *Linaria maroccana* 'Licilia Violet'.

Trees are useful for adding height and volume, especially in a small space. With an open canopy, a multistemmed *Elaeagnus* 'Quicksilver' filters the light, its silvery foliage reflecting it back into the garden.

Briza media is a low-growing grass with gleaming buds that catch the light. The seedpods, which quickly follow the flowers, last throughout autumn and sometimes into winter.

Clay pavers laid in a herringbone pattern appear to fragment where the path and plants meet.

Creamy lemon, vanilla and pink repeat throughout the garden.

The vanilla-coloured flowers of *Eschscholzia californica* 'Ivory Castle' beam out like lights, offsetting the darker colours of the design. Their simple, open flowers offer a long season of accessible pollen and nectar.

Featured plants

Foeniculum vulgare 'Purpureum' ★ **bronze fennel**

Papaver somniferum ★ **opium poppy**

Papaver somniferum 'Lauren's Grape' ★ **opium poppy**

Rosa 'Cardinal de Richelieu' ★ **rose**

Thalictrum 'Elin' ★ **meadow rue**

Thymus 'Fragrantissimus' ★ **orange-scented thyme**

A dash of red provided by the poppy *Papaver somniferum* 'Lauren's Grape' adds some colour and brightness against a largely green backdrop.

Colour breaks [5]

Aspect Sun
Soil Loam

Strong colour breaks and repeating patterns are key to this small, immersive space designed by Conrad Batten, which uses the light and dark tones of a limited colour palette. The dark fuzz provided by the foliage of *Foeniculum vulgare* 'Purpureum' (bronze fennel) is echoed in the dark centres of the *Papaver somniferum* (poppy) flowers and the narrow, inky stems of *Thalictrum* 'Elin' (meadow rue). Low-growing, boxy plants such as *Thymus* (thyme) are as useful for the empty space above them as the room they take up at ground level, letting sunlight into the garden. High above the other plants, the small, white flowers of *Thalictrum* 'Elin' catch and reflect the light.

In this garden, petal, leaf, stem and bud colour have all been carefully considered and, among the textural foliage, the pops of colour shine. Note that the poppy is doing double-duty, as both colourful flower and later seedpod.

- Atmosphere is created by the colours of the plants and the way they are used. A repeating palette ties the garden together, as the eye travels between plants of similar hues.

- In a small space, the choice of materials is important. A pale gravel path gives the impression of a pool of sunlight and feels in keeping with the garden's style.

- Plants fill all the available space and spill over their boundaries, blurring the point at which the plants and the paths meet.

- Using a mixture of long-flowering plants and transient flowers, such as poppies, exaggerates seasonal change, so there is always something new to see. Post-flowering, poppies and thalictrums have decorative seedheads that will endure throughout the winter.

- It may feel counterintuitive to feature big plants in a small space. But tall plants draw the eye upwards as well as making room for lower layers of plants.

Rosa 'Cardinal de Richlieu' repeats the pink of the opium poppy but in a darker hue.

Opposite: *Thymus* 'Fragrantissimus' (orange-scented thyme)

The small, white flowers of *Thalictrum* 'Elin' catch the light.

Papaver somniferum (opium poppy) with its delicate, pink flower.

The dark stems of *Thalictrum* 'Elin' and *Foeniculum vulgare* 'Purpureum' reference the dark blotch at the base of the petals of *Papaver somniferum*.

Pops of red [6]

Aspect Sun
Soil Loam

This small garden for a city-centre, ground-floor apartment, designed by Tony Woods of Garden Club London, includes separate areas for eating and relaxing. These are tied together by plants specifically chosen to draw wildlife into the space.

Red is a colour that works best when used in small amounts due to its ability to draw attention to itself. Here, it links the two parts of the garden. *Salvia* 'Royal Bumble' (sage) and *Callistemon citrinus* 'Splendens' (crimson bottlebrush) both stand out for their vivid red flowers, which jostle at close quarters, tempered by the silver-green foliage of plants such as *Echinops bannaticus* 'Taplow Blue' (globe thistle) and *Stipa tenuissima* (Mexican feather grass). Under the dappled light cast by two *Betula nigra* (black birch) trees, the garden feels like a hidden retreat.

Flowers that are small in scale, and not too far removed from the flower shapes found in nature, offer easy access to pollen and nectar for bees, butterflies and hoverflies.

In a small outdoor space, simplicity is key. Pale-coloured gravel and paving delineate the area for a table and chairs and accentuate the colours of the plants.

The view from the windows of the apartment has been kept as open as possible, seamlessly extending the living space and inviting nature in.

Featured plants

Betula nigra ★ **black birch**

Callistemon citrinus 'Splendens' ★ **crimson bottlebrush**

Crocosmia Orange Pekoe ('Pek Or') ★ **montbretia**

Echinops bannaticus 'Taplow Blue' ★ **globe thistle**

Salvia 'Royal Bumble' ★ **sage**

Stipa tenuissima ★ **Mexican feather grass**

- Where space is limited, the choice of furniture is even more important. The clean lines and muted colours of the contemporary furniture in this garden are in keeping with the modern architecture of the house and its urban location, as well as providing a foil for the plants.

- A limited colour palette creates a unified and harmonious vibe. The colours used are not of equal pegging – in this garden, red, appearing only in measured amounts, injects energy without becoming overwhelming.

- Plants with simple, open-centred flowers, such as salvias and crocosmias (montbretia), are the most beneficial for pollinators like bees, hoverflies and butterflies. Super long-flowering, they offer a continuous supply of pollen and nectar from the beginning of summer.

- In an urban setting, moving plants into the middle of a space shifts sightlines, increasing the feeling of being immersed in nature.

A firepit doubles up as a table, flanked by low-slung chairs. The garden is planted with a rich variety of textures, using plants of differing heights. The simple lines and dark colour of the chairs and firepit enhance rather than distract from the colours of the plants.

The glowing flowers of *Salvia* 'Royal Bumble' add a dash of red that is picked up by the aptly named bottlebrush flowers of *Callistemon citrinus* 'Splendens'.

Cor-Ten steel edging marks the edge of the path, keeping the planting in check. Tall plants make the most of the narrow space.

The plants are key to the design of the space, defining the layout as much as the paving and paths.

Callistemon citrinus 'Splendens' (crimson bottlebrush)

Betula nigra (black birch)

Echinops bannaticus 'Taplow Blue' (globe thistle)

The flower yard 7

Aspect Sun
Soil General-purpose compost

Small-space gardener Arthur Parkinson is known for his brilliance with colour. With no soil to work with, his big backyard containers are arranged in groups and filled with plants to make a garden. The scheme is purposefully limited to a narrow band of saturated colours, with the same plants repeating in multiple containers. There is an emphasis on single, open-centred flowers that are beneficial to pollinators. Plants with blackcurrant, crimson and fire-engine red flowers, including *Dahlia* 'Roxy', *Cosmos bipinnatus* 'Rubenza' and *Gladiolus* 'Magma', meld together and meet at their tips to make a garden that is more than the sum of its parts.

Creating colourful containers relies not only on flower colour but also on foliage. The green leaves of *Salvia* 'Amistad' (sage) and crimson-black foliage of *Dahlia* 'Waltzing Matilda' sit easily in this dark and rich palette.

As a general rule, the bigger the pot, the bigger the eventual plant will grow. One large pot with two or more plants has much more visual impact than several small containers and is also easier to look after in terms of frequency of watering. Dolly tubs and galvanized-metal troughs look great in any outdoor space. Painted blue, the backdrop to the containers complements their colours.

Featured plants

Cosmos bipinnatus 'Rubenza' ★ **cosmos**

Dahlia 'Bishop of Llandaff' ★ **dahlia**

Dahlia 'Roxy' ★ **dahlia**

Dahlia 'Waltzing Matilda' ★ **dahlia**

Gladiolus 'Magma' ★ **gladioli**

Salvia 'Amistad' ★ **sage**

- For maximum impact, large containers are gathered together, allowing their contents to meet and tumble together.

- The colour scheme for one or more containers can be planned in the same way as any small garden, by starting with a favourite plant and working outwards using the colours of its petals, stems, foliage and the centres of its flowers to build up a scheme.

- Crimson *Cosmos bipinnatus* 'Rubenza' matches the purple of *Salvia* 'Amistad' at the base of its petals, and the same colour repeats in the centre of the flowers of *Dahlia* 'Waltzing Matilda'. The cosmos and dahlia share a common red hue in differing amounts.

- The indigo calyces (flower bases) of *Salvia* 'Amistad' are as useful as its purple trumpet flower – they continue to contribute to the colours in the garden even after the flowers have faded.

- Choosing containers made from a common material creates a cohesive feel. Galvanized metal weathers beautifully, is easy to source and also relatively lightweight, even when planted.

- Creating a container that is brimful of colour depends not only on the choice of plants but also on the planting density. For a container, double the number of plants per square metre (10 square feet) that you would use in a garden bed or border.

The vibrant flowers of *Salvia* 'Amistad' burst from a galvanized metal planter.

Opposite: *Dahlia* 'Bishop of Llandaff'

From left to right: *Salvia* 'Amistad', *Dahlia* 'Waltzing Matilda' and *Cosmos bipinnatus* 'Rubenza'.

Thoughtful design and well-chosen, colourful plants can transform the space in front of your house.

Front gardens

The importance of front gardens

In the city where I live, 'Good Garden' awards are given to anyone with a front garden that enhances the neighbourhood. A beautiful space at the front of a house is often described as a 'gift to the street', acknowledging that its benefits extend beyond the person who made it. Yet, according to the Royal Horticultural Society, over the last two decades, more than 39,000 square kilometres (15,000 square miles) of front gardens have been paved over and lost to parking and bin storage in the UK.

Where space is limited, it is easy to overlook the potential of a well-planned front garden to improve everyday life by boosting mood and inspiring community pride. Even a few plants can improve local air quality by reducing the carbon dioxide from traffic fumes and lower the risk of flash flooding by allowing rainwater to seep steadily into the soil. Plants also help to counter what is described as the 'urban heat island effect', which makes towns and cities hotter at night than they should be.

From a shady front garden with ferns, grasses and seasonal bulbs to a sunny space planted in builder's rubble and a London design with a dreamy quality, here are five inspiring ideas for outside the front door.

In this combination, orange *Geum* 'Alabama Slammer' (avens) pairs beautifully with creamy-hued *Verbascum* 'Cotswold Cream' (mullein), which repeats the colour of the geum's petals in the centres of its flowers.

Deschampsia cespitosa (tufted hair grass) has an ethereal quality that, in combination with *Digitalis parviflora* (small-flowered foxglove), adds depth to the scheme. The dark colour of the corrugated fence serves to highlight the colours of the flowers.

Windowsill garden

Aspect Shade
Soil Loam

The garden-like atmosphere created by using the narrow windowsills outside this first-floor apartment demonstrates that no space is too small for colour.

Two windows are matched by pairs of containers that mirror each other in both their style and contents. Densely planted, they are overflowing with foliage and flowers, making them look well established and creating impact right from the start. The ferns *Asplenium scolopendrium* (hart's tongue fern), *Dryopteris filix-mas* 'Crispa Cristata' (male fern) and *Cyrtomium falcatum* (Japanese holly fern), plus the evergreen perennial *Farfugium japonicum* 'Wavy Gravy' (leopard plant), provide the foliage.

Well-chosen combinations of spring-flowering bulbs – namely tulips and daffodils – in an intentionally pared-back colour palette are repeated in all four containers, tying the scheme together like a little garden in miniature. Designer Colin Stewart's colour scheme takes its cue from the stripy tulips, *Tulipa* 'Marilyn' and *T.* 'Estrella Rijnveld', which are highlighted by the vibrant green *Euphorbia amygdaloides* 'Purpurea' (wood spurge). Their red stripes repeat in a darker tone in *T.* 'Slawa', while a pale, bunch-flowering daffodil, *Narcissus* 'Thalia', and *N.* 'Sailboat' pick up on their white.

The materials from which the containers are made and their decorative embellishments match the colour of the brickwork and the architecture of the building.

In an inspired twist, the colours in the containers chime with those in the interior of the apartment, including the blinds (window shades), the tablecloth and a bright red potted pelargonium. In addition, the blinds and cushions repeat the stripy theme of the plants.

- Generously planted containers on a windowsill will obscure the view from the street as well as make the experience of looking out through the window more enjoyable.

- In a small outdoor space, flowering bulbs in containers are an easy way to highlight the changing seasons.

- The containers are densely packed with plants, so their foliage and flowers completely cover the soil, but there is enough space in between for them to express their natural shapes.

- The colours and patterns on the windowsills are emphasized by elements of the interior, including a colourful Le Grand Etourdi mobile in front of the windows, the vibrant green of the table lamp, stripy cushions and a brilliant red pelargonium.

Tulipa 'Rococo' (tulip)

Euphorbia amygdaloides 'Purpurea'
★ **wood spurge**

Narcissus 'Thalia'
★ **daffodil**

Tulipa 'Estrella Rijnveld'
★ **tulip**

Amelanchier lamarckii
★ snowy mespilus

Dryopteris wallichiana
★ alpine wood fern

Shady space

Aspect Shade
Soil Loam

Front gardens often benefit from a lighter touch, in terms of design and upkeep. This north-facing garden uses colourful seasonal bulbs, woven among evergreen ferns and grasses in various shades of green. The grass *Luzula nivea* (snowy wood-rush) has umbels of tiny, white flowers reminiscent of cow parsley. It is understated enough to use among a wide range of bulbs, drawing out their wilder aesthetics.

Planted beneath an *Amelanchier lamarckii* (snowy mespilus), the flowering of the tulips coincides with the bursting of its blossom. They are first in a procession of bulbs that flower throughout the year. A small tree like this can create privacy in a front garden, obscuring sightlines from the street.

A trio of tulips – here *Tulipa* 'Spring Green', *T.* 'Ballerina' and *T.* 'Brown Sugar' – is a good opportunity to play with colour. While most tulips flower only once, the first two in this trio are reliably perennial. Once in the soil, they will return to flower each spring. They are followed later in summer by towering *Fritillaria* (fritillary) and *Lilium martagon* (Turk's cap lily).

- Plant spring-flowering bulbs like tulips and fritillaries in autumn and summer-flowering bulbs such as Turk's cap lilies at the end of winter. Instead of arranging bulbs in rigid patterns, aim to create pools of colour, mimicking the way plants arrange themselves in the nature.

- The leaves of bulbs need to remain in place post-flowering to replenish the bulbs' resources for flowering again next spring. Pairing tulips with evergreen ferns and grasses means the leaves are lost among their foliage.

Hakonechloa macra
★ Japanese forest grass

Tulipa 'Spring Green'
★ tulip

Tulipa 'Ballerina'
★ tulip

Allium hollandicum 'Purple Sensation'
★ **Dutch garlic**

Salvia nemorosa 'Caradonna'
★ **Balkan clary**

Dianthus carthusianorum
★ **carthusian pink**

Colour in rubble

Aspect Sun
Soil Builder's rubble

Pairing informality with sharp colour, this city-centre front garden, designed by Ed O'Brien, uses the mercurial qualities of plants to its advantage. The emergent foliage of *Stipa gigantea* (golden oats) and *Seslaria autumnalis* (autumn moor-grass) provide a green undercurrent to tiny-flowered, summer-flowering perennials, including dark violet *Salvia nemorosa* 'Caradonna' (Balkan clary) and neon-pink *Dianthus carthusianorum* (carthusian pink). Held on a scaffold of tall, narrow stems, the small, lilac flowers of *Verbena bonariensis* (purple top) hover above the spent flowers of alliums – now pinky-hued seedheads – which are architectural and robust enough to last throughout winter. What might, on first observation, appear to be a very colourful palette is actually a series of graduated colours.

Simple flower shapes that are not too far removed from those found in nature offer a degree of transparency, so the sunlight filters through and illuminates the scheme. The garden is planted into builder's rubble, recycled following building work. Despite this, the 3 x 3m (10 x 10ft) space has layers of detail and colour that change throughout the year.

- Consider what the plants will contribute even after they have passed their traditional best. Alliums, for example, have architectural seedheads that are robust enough to last into autumn and winter.

- Using perennial plants, such as salvias and *Dianthus carthusianorum*, along with reliably perennial bulbs that flower every year, like alliums, helps to keep the maintenance of this front garden to a minimum.

Seslaria autumnalis
★ autumn moor-grass

Stipa gigantea
★ golden oats

Verbena bonariensis
★ purple top

Sphaeralcea 'Newleaze Coral' (globe mallow)

Sphaeralcea (globe mallow)

Catananche caerulea (Cupid's dart)

Filmy colour

Aspect Sun
Soil Gravel

The colours in this city front garden have a dreamy quality that feels spontaneous, as if the plants have arranged themselves. There is a rhythm to how they rise and fall, and their colours catch the light. Yellow umbels of *Achillea* 'Moonshine' (yarrow) anchor the palette and are picked up in the bright yellow flowers of *Coreopsis verticillata* 'Moonbeam' (tickseed) and acid-yellow flowers of *Foeniculum vulgare* (common fennel). The star-like flowers of *Catananche caerulea* (Cupid's dart) appear to hover on their wiry stems, introducing blue, which is then repeated in a darker tone in the two purple alliums: lilac-blue *Allium* 'Millennium' (ornamental onion) and darker-hued *A. sphaerocephalon* (drumstick allium). The spacing between the plants feels intentional and allows a glimpse of what lies beyond.

The design brief for this garden was to include as much colour as possible to create a wild and informal space, and designer Marc O'Neill chose to use plants replete with small flowers, which draw a wide range of pollinators into the space. At the front of the property, the garden benefits the whole community as well as the artist who lives there.

A woven hazel boundary amplifies rather than distracts from the colours of the plants.

- Use a limited palette of colours to create a cohesive scheme and repeat the same plants throughout the space.

- Yellow *Achillea* 'Moonshine' and orange *A.* 'Terracotta' anchor the planting, which includes shots of glowing colour from the flowers of *Sphaeralcea* 'Newleaze Coral' (globe mallow) and dusky purple *Allium sphaerocephalon*. The dark, bobble seedheads of *Echinacea purpurea* (purple coneflower) repeat the shape of the allium flowers and the inky centres of the yellow, daisy-like flowers of *Rudbeckia triloba* (brown-eyed Susan).

- Include tall plants such as *Verbena bonariensis* (purple top) alongside shorter plants like *Coreopsis* to create a dynamic, layered look that allows light to fall between them and play on their colours.

- Plants with myriad small, open-centred flowers are the most helpful for pollinators. Using plants such as *Sphaeralcea* (globe mallow) and achilleas boosts biodiversity as well as ensuring continuous colour.

- Colours rarely clash in nature. Using plants with colours on a sliding scale, such as achillea and *Coreopsis* or verbena and *Allium hollandicum* 'Purple Sensation' (Dutch garlic), creates harmony in a garden while feeling free and uninhibited.

Bold dashes of colour provided by yellow *Achillea* 'Moonshine' and orange *A.* 'Terracotta' dominate the planting scheme but are punctuated by the brighter colours and contrasting shapes of pale purple *Allium sphaerocephalon* and the dark purple English lavender *Lavandula angustifolia* Blue Spear ('Pas1213794').

Coreopsis verticillata 'Moonbeam' and *Achillea* 'Terracotta' are enlivened by lilac *Sphaeralcea* and blue *Catanache caerulea*.

The colours of *Verbena bonariensis* and *Foeniculum vulgare* echo those of *Allium* 'Millennium' and *Achillea* 'Moonshine', respectively.

Room for a car

Aspect Sun
Soil Builder's rubble

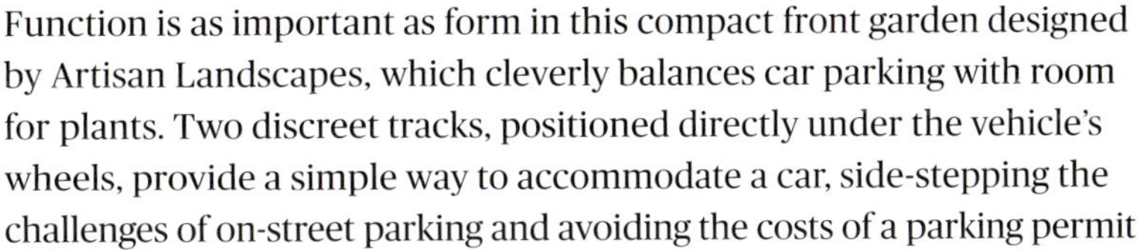

Function is as important as form in this compact front garden designed by Artisan Landscapes, which cleverly balances car parking with room for plants. Two discreet tracks, positioned directly under the vehicle's wheels, provide a simple way to accommodate a car, side-stepping the challenges of on-street parking and avoiding the costs of a parking permit.

Grey, rectangular pavers, arranged in a geometric pattern, and pale gravel provide the backdrop for plants in repeating colours, which are robust enough to withstand the occasional car tyre.

Plants with small flowers, such as *Lavandula angustifolia* (English lavender), *Thymus vulgaris* (common thyme) and *Erigeron karvinskianus* (Mexican fleabane), blur the point where pavers and planting meet, as well as benefitting a wide variety of pollinators. With its spring blossom and light summer canopy, the *Amelanchier lamarckii* (snowy mespilus) tree obscures the view of the car from the windows of the house, while still allowing the light to filter though its branches.

In the space adjacent to the parking spot, the garden shifts gear and is imbued with a wilder vibe. A curving path indicates the way to the front door, flanked by purple *Salvia nemorosa* 'Caradonna' (Balkan clary) and the cranesbill *Geranium* Rozanne ('Gerwat'), white veronicastrums and green grasses that all stay true to the garden's narrow tonal palette.

- In the UK, permission is required if you want vehicular access from the street. Planning consent is also needed for hardstanding areas that are larger than 5 square metres (54 square feet), unless these are made from permeable materials.

- The tracks for parking should be 300–600mm (12–24in) wide; wider tracks will make parking easier.

- Lavender is a wonderful plant in a narrow space. It is resilient to bumps, releases a delicious scent when brushed against and can easily be cut back to fit the space.

- Plants such as lavender and *Geranium* Rozanne ('Gerwat') are of particular benefit to pollinators. The colour of their flowers is often described as 'bee-blue' because it draws insects such as bees that can see ultraviolet light.

Opposite: *Lavandula angustifolia* 'Hidcote', *L. a.* 'Loddon Pink' and *Erigeron karvinskianus* make this garden a hub for pollinators.

Thymus vulgaris, *T. serpyllum* (wild thyme) and *Erigeron karvinskianus* soften the transition between hardstanding areas and paths, as well as attracting pollinators.

Veronicastrum virginicum 'Album' (Culver's root)

Geranium Rozanne ('Gerwat') (cranesbill)

Erigeron karvinskianus (Mexican fleabane)

Where soil and space are limited, a thoughtfully planted container can transform even the smallest space, adding texture and vibrant colour.

Colour in containers

Getting started

A beautifully planted container has the capacity to improve even the smallest outdoor space, transforming a shady side return, the space next to a doorway or the beginning of a path into natural stopping points. In a very small space, a tabletop pot can be enjoyed from inside and out, setting the tone of both the house and garden.

A well-placed small plant in a small pot is emphasized by prominent placement, so bring it into the limelight, and where soil is limited a thoughtfully arranged collection of good-sized containers in a colourful scheme is enough to create a garden.

- Think of a container as a garden-in-miniature and select the plants in the usual way. Choose one plant as a starting point and use the colours of its flowers – the petals and centres, the foliage and the colour of the stems – as building blocks to create a scheme.

- If you are planning to use more than one container, think about how they will sit together. A mixture of different shapes and sizes of container in a common material works well, as does a group of identical containers.

- Match the scale of the container to the size of the plant and pick one that is large enough to support it and allows for root growth. Keep like plants with like, in terms of compost and watering requirements, to ensure the plants thrive.

- Pay attention to the colour of the background to the container, including the play of shadow and light. The backdrop against which the container is set should complement it and elevate the plants it holds.

- Pairing containers made from urban or industrial materials with free-flowing, layered plants feels very modern in a city setting.

Place containers in a prominent position to create impact (opposite) or close by for easy care (above).

Tips for planting containers

Almost any vessel can be used as a container, but you may need to make drainage holes in the base or add a few centimetres of horticultural grit beneath the compost to prevent waterlogging – plants don't like sitting in wet compost. Also, once a large container has been planted, it will be heavy and difficult to move, so position it in its final spot before filling it with compost and planting it up.

The success of the container depends on both the choice of plants and the planting density. Use a mix of taller and shorter plants to create layers, planting with half the amount of space between them than you would in a border. When planting bulbs, the general rule is to use the same number per pot as the width of the pot in centimetres. For example, 20 tulip bulbs in a pot measuring 20cm (8in) across.

Container-grown plants are totally reliant on you to provide water and nutrients. Feed the plants weekly during the summer, using a liquid seaweed feed or diluted organic tomato food. Be prepared to water daily in sunny or windy conditions, even if it rains. When watering, direct the water jet at the compost and the plant roots rather than the flowers and foliage. Ideally, water in the morning or evening, as this allows the plants to absorb the moisture away from the heat of the day.

Mulch pots with a layer of grit to cover the soil, retain moisture and prevent smaller plants from getting splashed with compost when it rains.

Compost

As a consequence of our better understanding of the need to preserve peatlands as carbon stores and for the vital habitats they provide for wildlife, peat is no longer included in bagged compost. Instead, it might contain wood fibre, bark, composted green waste or coir, and different brands use these materials in varying amounts.

It is helpful to think of a bag of compost as just one of the ingredients in the compost 'recipe' for a container and a base to which you can add others. Add a few scoops of horticultural grit for a plant that needs good drainage, for example, or a scoop of garden soil for substance and heft. You can even include old, spent compost from a previously planted container if you have some.

Note that without the churn of worms and soil microbes, garden soil on its own is best avoided, as it quickly becomes empty of organic life.

To benefit plants, the compost in a container needs to contain moisture and air and have a fibrous fee, vital and full of life.

Bear in mind that bagged compost has a shelf-life, so only buy the amount you need and use it fresh. Check the manufacturing date printed on the bag: if it was made more than six months ago, its biological properties will have changed, reducing its effectiveness.

Consider the contents of a bag of compost as just one ingredient in a container compost recipe.

Metallic tones

The tall, quirky line of a yellow *Verbascum bombyciferum* (mullein) sets the tone in this asymmetrically planted galvanized metal tub (diameter 36cm/14in). A staggered mix of buds and flowers that make their way to the top of the flower spike and the exaggerated size of its foliage, which extends beyond the lip of the pot, hint at a spontaneous combination, as if the plants have sown themselves in the container.

The verbascum, mathiasella, poppy and coleus all have foliage or flowers with hints of blue, which play off each other as well as the metallic silver-blue of the tub. *Papaver rupifragum* (perennial poppy) is an exceptionally long-flowering poppy with electric-orange flowers – it is a perennial and so will return to flower every year.

Big galvanized metal tubs are easy to find online or in salvage yards. Don't skimp on the size of the container, though, as larger containers need watering less often because they hold on to water better.

Verbascum bombyciferum
★ **mullein**
Tall spires of yellow flowers and big, felty, grey-blue foliage

Mathiasella bupleuroides 'Green Dream'
★ **mathiasella**
Super long-lasting, green umbel flowers that are tinged pink at their tips

Papaver rupifragum
★ **perennial poppy**
A perennial poppy with glaucous green foliage and delicate, bright tangerine flowers

Coleus argentatus 'Silver Shield'
★ **coleus**
Silver-blue leaves that are violet on their reverse and held on muted purple stems. Bears small, white flowers later in summer.

1
Water the plants thoroughly in their original nursery pots – the water should run out of the holes in the bottom. Drill a few holes in the base of the tub (if there aren't some there already).

2
Position the tub in a warm, sunny spot, as it will be difficult to move once it is full of compost.

3
Fill the tub almost to the rim with general-purpose compost, leaving a few centimetres between the lip of the tub and the top of the compost for watering.

4
Start with the *Verbascum bombyciferum,* positioning it slightly off-centre in the tub. Next, add the *Mathiasella bupleuroides* 'Green Dream' and *Coleus argentatus* 'Silver Shield, followed by the two *Papaver rupifragram*, leaving enough space between the plants to allow them to grow.

5
When you are happy with the composition, tip each plant out of its pot, loosen a few of the roots with your fingertips and plant in the tub, making sure they are at the same depth in the compost as they were in their original pots.

6
Fill the gaps between the plants with additional compost, using your hands to gently press it down and secure the plants in place.

7
Water the compost thoroughly in order to settle it around the roots of the plants.

Two-tone tub

Bicoloured flowers always have a slightly kitsch feel, and here the two-tone *Salvia* Amethyst Lips ('Dyspurp') takes centre stage in a heavy, iron tub (diameter 30cm/12in). The flowers of all four of the plants in this scheme vary on a scale of blues, with the small, snapdragon-like flowers of *Linaria maroccana* 'Licilia Violet' (Moroccan toadflax) at the darker end of the spectrum and *Penstemon heterophyllus* 'Electric Blue' at the lightest. The white flecks at the tips of the salvia's flowers inject vibrancy and lift the scheme, preventing it from feeling flat. The salvia, linaria and penstemon share a narrow, upright habit and similarly small, scant leaves and so sit easily together in terms of overall 'feel'. *Baptisia* 'Dutch Chocolate' (false indigo), which is also two-tone, picks up on the rusty brown hue of the tub.

The blocky shape of the tub and its brown patina contrast well with the airy forms of the plants, anchoring them and almost making it look as if they are growing directly in soil.

Baptisia 'Dutch Chocolate'
★ **false indigo**
Rich, dark blooms with a chocolate hue

Penstemon heterophyllus 'Electric Blue'
★ **penstemon**
Vibrant blue flowers with a striking, electric tone

Linaria maroccana 'Licilia Violet'
★ **Moroccan toadflax**
Small, violet, snapdragon-like flowers

Salvia Amethyst Lips ('Dyspurp')
★ **sage**
Bright amethyst flowers marked with white

1
Keeping the plants in their original pots to begin with, water each one thoroughly until water runs out the holes in the bottom.

2
Prepare the tub by drilling a few holes in the base (if necessary) and position in a warm, sunny spot that ideally receives some shade for part of the day. This will prevent it drying out too quickly.

3
Fill the base of the tub with a few centimetres of horticultural grit and then fill with a mixture of general-purpose compost and grit, leaving enough room for watering later.

4
Arrange the plants in the tub, keeping them in their pots at first, so you can adjust the composition. Start with the *Baptisia* 'Dutch Chocolate', placing it in the centre, then tuck in the *Salvia* Amethyst Lips ('Dyspurp') and *Penstemon heterophyllus* 'Electric Blue' around it. Position the *Linaria maroccana* 'Licilia Violet' slightly to one side, monitoring the balance of the arrangement. Keep some space between the plants – the aim is to highlight their shapes.

5
Tip each plant out of its pot, loosen a few roots with your fingertips and plant in the tub at the same depth as it was in its original pot. Fill the gaps between the plants with more compost before gently firming in.

6
Water the compost well to settle it around the plants' roots. You can also add a thin layer of grit to the top of the compost for a finished look.

Nature's colours

In a small garden, a simple design that relies on just two plant genera can be more effective than a busy display. This colourful ceramic container (diameter 34cm/13in) for a tabletop leans into nature, using plants with small flowers that will continue to look good for weeks, if not months, with very little effort. The daisy-like flowers of *Erigeron karvinskianus* (Mexican fleabane) provide a subtle understorey for the delicate, pink umbels of *Tulbaghia violacea* (society garlic), which turn prettily outwards at their tips, and white *T.* 'Hoyland Chameleon'. The occasional pink flower thrown up by the *Erigeron* and the pink markings on the tips of its white flowers tie the two genera together beautifully to create a harmonious combination.

The pale green of the container is complemented by the colour of the table, while its low, shallow shape balances the heights and forms of the plants. The simple, low design also allows the plants to take centre stage.

Erigeron karvinskianus
★ **Mexican fleabane**
A mass of white, daisy-like flowers with yellow button centres and the occasional pink flower

Tulbaghia violacea
★ **society garlic**
Pink umbel flowers on narrow green stems and narrow foliage

1
Keeping the plants in their original pots to begin with, water each one well until water runs out the holes in the bottom.

2
Tip a scoop of horticultural grit into the base of the container and fill with general-purpose compost, leaving a space between the top of the compost and the rim of the container for watering.

3
Tap the plants out of their pots. What is important is the overall composition, with the narrow uprights emerging from the low filler plants. Position two pink *Tulbaghia violacea* next to each other in the centre of the container. Plant a white *Tulbaghia* 'Hoyland Chameleon' towards the back. Tuck two *Erigeron karvinskianus* in around the other plants, packing them in so the flowers and foliage cover the surface of the compost.

4
When you are happy with the composition, loosen a few of the plants' roots with your fingertips, scoop out holes in the compost and plant each one. Keep the plants at the same depth as they were in their nursery pots.

5
Carefully firm the compost around each plant to ensure good root contact but without compacting it too much.

6
Water the pot thoroughly and stand it on a table, ideally somewhere it will be in the sun for most of the day.

Beauty in simplicity

This clay pot (diameter 33cm/13in) contains plants that all grow at similar rates. They share a similarly airy habit, but differ in flower shape. White is a recurring theme: in the small flowers of *Salvia* 'Phyllis Fancy' (sage), the petal markings of *S. patens* 'Dot's Delight' (gentian sage) and as a base hue in the pink petals of *Dahlia merckii* (Merck dahlia). The colourful calyxces of the blue salvia are very long-lasting and will continue to add colour even after the flowers fade.

The dark colour of the dahlia stems is echoed in those of *S.* 'Phyllis Fancy' and again in the grey-brown of the pot. The pot's upright shape mirrors the design of the composition and is large enough to support the plants and accommodate their roots. Its muted tone doesn't distract from the vibrant flower colours. The pretty foliage of *D. merckii* contributes to the tiered effect and softens the transition between pot and plants. With flowers that resemble those in nature, the plants are ideal for pollinators.

Salvia patens 'Dot's Delight'
★ **gentian sage**
A compact salvia with tubular flowers, marked with white

Salvia 'Phyllis Fancy'
★ **sage**
Tall, airy plant with white-tipped, purple, tubular flowers and navy calyxces

Dahlia merckii
★ **Merck dahlia**
Fresh pink flowers with contrasting yellow middles

1
Sown in spring, some perennials – like *Dahlia merckii* – flower in their first year and so it makes sense to grow them from seed rather than buying them in.

2
To ensure flowering takes place as soon as possible, sow the seed in early spring, then prick out the seedlings into a small pot and keep on a sunny windowsill. This will protect the young plants from frost and ensure they are big enough to plant outside in late spring.

3
Choose a pot that is deep enough to support the plants. Ensure it has proper drainage – if there are no holes in the base, then you will need to drill some yourself.

4
Stand the pot somewhere that is warm and sunny for most of the day. Fill almost to the rim with general-purpose compost and horticultural grit. Water the plants in their original pots thoroughly.

5
Position the plants – one *Salvia patens* 'Dot's Delight', two *S.* 'Phyllis Fancy' and three *Dahlia merckii* – in the pot in a triangular layout; aim to create an informal rather than structured design.

6
Make holes in the compost and plant up the pot, ensuring the plants are at the same depth as they were in their original pots. Use more compost to fill any gaps and gently firm in. Water well, avoiding splashing the foliage. The compost needs to be evenly moist but not waterlogged.

As long as it is suited to the soil and the amount of sun or shade in your garden, any plant can be the inspiration for its design. Here are my Top 40 plants for colour.

Top 40

Annuals and biennials

An annual is a plant that completes its lifecycle in one year and doesn't grow back the following year. Sown from seed, it germinates, produces shoots and flowers within 12 months.

Annuals are described as either 'hardy' or 'half-hardy'. A hardy annual is a plant that is resilient to cold temperatures and can survive frost. A half-hardy annual is one that is vulnerable to frost and dislikes cold and wet conditions. Whether a plant is hardy makes a difference to the timing of the sowing of its seeds and its subsequent planting outside.

A biennial is a plant that completes its lifecycle in two years. Sown from seed, it germinates and grows roots and leaves in year one and then flowers in year two.

- Annuals and biennials are easily grown from seed and this, coupled with the fact that they grow quickly, makes growing them from scratch the best option. Sown in spring, an annual will be in flower by mid-summer. You can also sow seeds in autumn for bigger plants that will start flowering a few weeks earlier the following year.

- Contemporary schemes tend to use fewer plants in greater numbers, and the low cost of a packet of seeds, which will potentially produce lots of plants, makes this a viable option. The affordability of annuals and biennials means you can grow them in an uninhibited way, allowing you to experiment and refine your selection to find the colours you like best.

- Most annuals and some biennials set a lot of seed and, in the case of plants like *Verbena bonariensis* (purple top) and *Cerinthe major* 'Purpurascens' (honeywort), the seedlings will grow into plants that are identical to the original, giving them a permanent presence in the garden.

- Biennials are invaluable because they bloom in late spring after bulbs such as tulips and before most annuals and perennials, filling what gardeners call 'the hungry gap' between late spring and early summer.

Annuals, such as *Papaver commutatum* 'Ladybird' (poppy), are quick and easy to grow from seed.

Latin name	*Cerinthe major* 'Purpurascens'
Common name	**honeywort**
★	hardy annual
Sow	early to late spring, early to mid-autumn
Plant	early to late spring
Flowers	late spring to early autumn

height – 30cm (12in)
spacing – 3 per m^2 ($10ft^2$)
soil – well drained
aspect – sun

This captivating annual has small, violet flowers, tipped in white and encased in bracts that shift from green to deep blue. The colour of the bracts deepens in the heat of the sun, eventually turning purple. Its glaucous leaves are speckled in white and the petioles (leaf stalks) are red-pink. Its cultivar name – 'Purpurascens' – translates from the Latin as 'becoming purple', which is an apt description. The flowers and foliage are a big draw for pollinators, particularly bees during summer. Once pollinated, the flowers evolve into chunky, jet-black seeds.

This annual revels in a sunny spot and pairs well with thyme, its blue and purple leaves and flowers contrasting with the herb's dense evergreen foliage. Unlike the cerinthe, the thyme makes a solid, compact shape. The blue tones of cerinthe are also lovely with *Pulsatilla vulgaris* (pasqueflower), a plant with violet flowers and later fluffy seedheads.

Sow seeds in pots of seed compost in spring or autumn, lightly cover and then keep outside.

Goes well with

Linaria maroccana 'Licilia Violet' (Moroccan toadflax)
Pulsatilla vulgaris (pasque flower)
Salvia 'Nachtvlinder' (sage)
Thymus 'Fragrantissimus' (orange-scented thyme)

Latin name	*Eschscholzia californica* 'Ivory Castle'
Common name	**California poppy**
★	hardy annual
Sow	early to late spring, early to mid-autumn
Plant	late spring to early summer
Flowers	early to late summer

height – 30cm (12in)
spacing – 3 per m^2 (10ft^2)
soil – any
aspect – sun

Despite being an annual, *Eschscholzia californica* 'Ivory Castle' will establish itself as a constant presence in your garden, as it is an eager self-sower. Delicate in appearance, its mother-of-pearl flowers have butter-yellow centres reminiscent of a poppy. They sit atop narrow, blue-green foliage, which forms a soft, low mound that complements the upright flower stems, adding a lovely texture to the garden. The flowers emerge from tight buds and, even when fully open, close again in the fading light, only to reopen in sun the following day. After flowering, this California poppy produces long seedpods that start green and then crack open with a snap to release their seeds, which germinate easily, to flower the following year. It is an immensely satisfying annual to grow, producing flowers generously in summer.

Sow seeds in pots of seed compost in spring or autumn, lightly cover and then keep outside.

Goes well with

Achillea 'Terracotta' (yarrow)
Cerinthe major 'Purpurascens' (honeywort)
Thymus 'Fragrantissimus' (orange-scented thyme)

Latin name	*Linaria maroccana* 'Licilia Violet'
Common name	**Moroccan toadflax**
★	hardy annual
Sow	early to late spring, early to mid-autumn
Plant	early to late spring
Flowers	early summer to mid-autumn

height – 50cm (20in)
spacing – 1 per m^2 ($10ft^2$)
soil – any
aspect – sun

This hardy annual has numerous tiny, snapdragon-like flowers held above narrow, green foliage. It is an excellent filler plant, creating a soft blur of colour. It pairs beautifully with *Salvia rosmarinus* (rosemary), with its lightly held flowers contrasting nicely with the rosemary's dark, needle-like foliage. The violet-blue colour of this toadflax is similar in depth and intensity to the rosemary's green. Additionally, *Orlaya grandiflora* (white laceflower) complements its ethereal quality.

Early-flowering, this hardy annual is useful for bridging the gap between early spring and summer flowers.

Sow seeds in pots of seed compost in spring or autumn, lightly cover and then keep outside. Grown from seed, *Linaria maroccana* 'Licilia Violet' flowers in record time – in just six weeks from sowing.

Goes well with

Orlaya grandiflora (white laceflower)
Papaver dubium subsp. *lecoqii* 'Albiflorum' (Beth's poppy)
Salvia rosmarinus (rosemary)
Tulbaghia violacea (society garlic)

Latin name	*Orlaya grandiflora* AGM
Common name	**white laceflower**
★	hardy annual
Sow	early to late spring, early to mid-autumn
Plant	early to late spring
Flowers	late spring to late summer

height – 60cm (24in)
spacing – 4 per m^2 ($10ft^2$)
soil – well drained, sandy
aspect – sun, partial shade

Delicate in appearance, with divided green leaves and large, intricately textured, white flowers, this is one of the most beautiful annuals and it has leapt into fashion recently with the swing towards a more natural style of gardening. Its airy habit makes it an excellent companion for many other plants and it is at its best used in number, weaving its way among them. Positioning this plant needs a little thought, however, as the empty space between its base and the flowers, where the light drops through, is easily lost if it is planted too densely. Use this annual to balance out heavier or more solid-looking plants, creating a visual contrast that enhances both. Like all white flowers, it looks most arresting early or late in the day, when its blooms appear to glow in the half-light. It is happiest in sun but can handle a little shade, making it useful for brightening up gloomy areas and creating a sense of lightness.

Sow seeds in pots of seed compost in spring or autumn, lightly cover and then keep outside.

Goes well with

Linaria maroccana 'Licilia Violet' (Moroccan toadflax)

Papaver dubium subsp. *lecoqii* 'Albiflorum' (Beth's poppy)

Latin name	*Papaver*
Common name	**annual poppy**
★	hardy annual
Sow	early to late spring, early to mid-autumn
Plant	early to late spring
Flowers	late spring to late summer; the architectural seedpods that follow the flowers last into winter

height – 50cm–1m (20–39in)
spacing – 3 per m^2 (10ft^2)
soil – well drained, sandy
aspect – sun

Annual poppies are useful for their heft and intense dollops of colour. Colourful in bud, bloom and seedpod, the glaucous buds break to reveal richly pigmented flowers. The petals are tissue-paper thin and so the flowers are almost over before they start, but they open in swift succession. Once the flowers have shed their petals, they are replaced by glaucous seedpods that are very robust and last throughout winter, turning grey and vanilla in cold weather.

Poppies work best planted in irregular patterns, so the eye skips from one to another, adding height and definition to a small space. Position them where the flowers will stand proud of other plants close by, so their petals catch and filter the light.

True pink *Papaver somniferum* (opium poppy) and blackcurrant-coloured *Papaver s.* 'Lauren's Grape' are both tall with thick-cut foliage that has quite a substantial presence in a small garden. Red *P. commutatum* 'Ladybird' pumps out colour strongly and each of its petals is marked with a black blotch. *P. dubium* subsp. *lecoqii* 'Albiflorum' (Beth's poppy) has delicate pink flowers with yellow centres and dark grey anthers and foliage that is almost as pretty as its flowers.

Annual poppies are swift and easy to grow from seed. Standard practice is to cast the seed directly onto the soil, but the seedlings are easily lost to slugs this way. Instead, sow a pinch of seed in seed compost in a cellular seed tray in spring or autumn, then prick out the plants swiftly before their roots fill the cells. This quick change of location avoids the root disturbance so disliked by annual poppies.

Goes well with

Dianthus carthusianorum (carthusian pink)
Salvia rosmarinus (rosemary)
Tulbaghia violacea (society garlic)

Far left: Opaque green seedpods replace the flowers from summer, turning milk-white in winter.

Left: Plant poppies such as *Papaver somniferum* 'Lauren's Grape' where the sun can illuminate their colours.

Latin name	*Verbascum bombyciferum* 'Polarsommer'
Common name	**mullein**
★	biennial
Sow	early to late spring, mid- to late summer
Plant	late spring to early summer
Flowers	late spring to early summer; the architectural seedpods that follow the flowers last into winter

height – 1.8m (6ft)
spacing – 1 per m^2 ($10ft^2$)
soil – well drained
aspect – sun

A staggered mix of buds and small flowers on a towering spike, this is one of the most useful plants for adding height and contributing to the layers of colour in a small space. The flowers open gradually, in shades of pale yellow, and in a compact spot just one plant is enough to carve up the space and create an upwards accent. Two or three plants, spaced irregularly, are even better, drawing the eye into the garden as it skips from one to the next. Plants with silver leaves can create a sense of space and serve as effective mediators between colours that might initially seem incompatible, blending diverse hues. It is also best grown in a spot where its flowers can catch the light, surrounded by shorter plants that won't overshadow its height.

A biennial plant, mullein should ideally be grown from seed, producing roots and foliage in its first year and flowering in its second. Or buy it as a young plant in a small pot if you want it to flower sooner.

Goes well with

Dianthus carthusianorum (carthusian pink)
Hakonechloa macra (Japanese forest grass)
Papaver commutatum 'Ladybird' (poppy)
Papaver somniferum 'Lauren's Grape' (opium poppy)

Perennials

A perennial is a plant that will flower year after year. Perennials are described as either 'woody' or 'herbaceous'. A woody perennial is a plant with woody stems. An herbaceous perennial is a plant that produces new stems and foliage each spring and then flowers, usually in summer. In winter it remains dormant under the soil.

- While some perennials will flower a few months after their seeds are sown, most are slower and are best bought as young plants in small pots.

- In comparison to sowing seed, buying a perennial plant in a pot has a quite a big carbon footprint to begin with, but it will only need planting once and from that point will grow on and on.

- Key to success is to buy a small plant in a 9cm (3½in) pot, which will settle more quickly in your garden than a bigger, more established plant.

- Unlike annuals and biennials, woody perennials such as *Salvia rosmarinus* (rosemary) are a year-round presence in the garden. Lots of herbaceous perennials, such as *Papaver rupifragrum* (perennial poppy), invest energy in creating strong and robust seedheads, often with beautiful architectural shapes, which will contribute to the colours in your garden even after the flowers fade.

- You can plant perennials at all times of year, except when the ground is frozen.

Perennial plants such as *Dianthus carthusianorum* (carthusian pink) flower year after year.

Latin name	*Achillea* 'Terracotta'
Common name	**yarrow**
★	perennial
Plant	early to mid-autumn
Flowers	early to late summer

height – 1m (39in)
spacing – 2 per m^2 ($10ft^2$)
soil – well drained
aspect – sun

In common with all yarrows, *Achillea* 'Terracotta' is prized in the garden for its mercurial colours. The flowers, which open with a toasted-orange colour and gradually turn yellow, unfurl sequentially on the same plant, to make a pretty mix of colours.

Achillea 'Terracotta' is best grown among plants that have a similarly architectural habit and makes a good choice for gravel gardens or those planted on builder's rubble. As a rule, achilleas are quite short-lived, but growing them in impoverished soil conditions can make them more reliable. The flat, open shape of their flowers is particularly useful for smaller pollinators.

Goes well with

Allium 'Millennium' (yarrow)
Catananche caerulea (Cupid's dart)

Latin name	*Anemone* Wild Swan ('Macane001')
Common name	**windflower**
★	perennial
Plant	early to mid-autumn
Flowers	late spring to late autumn; the cotton-wool-like seedheads last into winter

height – 45cm (18in)
spacing – 2 per m^2 ($10ft^2$)
soil – any
aspect – partial shade

A lovely, late-summer-flowering perennial, *Anemone* Wild Swan ('Macane001') is valued for its ability to prolong colour in the garden. The bright white flowers with orange centres are tinged with violet-blue and are a darker violet on the reverse during the summer. It pairs well with *Dahlia merckii* (Merck dahlia), complementing the dahlia's pink flowers, which have a base note of white, and referencing the yellow of their centres in its orange boss. It also works well with cool blues and purple, such as *Nepeta racemosa* 'Walker's Low' (catmint).

Towards winter the flowers turn into cotton-wool-like seedheads that last long after the flowers have faded. Despite its delicate appearance, this is a robust and resilient perennial, happily enduring the buffeting of wind and rain, which has the added bonus of revealing the colourful undersides of its flowers.

Goes well with

Dahlia merckii (Merck dahlia)
Nepeta racemosa 'Walker's Low' (catmint)
Nepeta 'Six Hills Giant' (catmint)

Latin name	*Asplenium scolopendrium* AGM
Common name	**hart's-tongue fern**
★	perennial (evergreen)
Latin name	*Dryopteris wallichiana* AGM
Common name	**alpine wood fern**
★	perennial (deciduous or semi-evergreen)
Plant	early spring to mid-autumn
Flowers	ferns are typically planted for their foliage

height – 60cm (24in)
spacing – 3 per m^2 ($10ft^2$)
soil – any
aspect – full shade, partial shade

An evergreen fern with glossy, sculptural leaves, *Asplenium scolopendrium*, commonly known as the hart's tongue fern, is valuable for its fresh, bright green in spring, its summer mid-green and its dark winter green. New, tongue-like fronds, which unfurl early in the year, pair well with wood ferns like *Dryoptris wallichiana* (alpine wood fern), the two plants working together to create tessellating patterns where their leaves overlap at the tips. The dense, rippling leaves of the hart's tongue fern offer weight in contrast to the wood fern's widely toothed, green foliage. This pairing is made even better with the addition of low-growing, clump-forming grasses like *Hakonechloa macra* (Japanese forest grass) and *Luzula nivea* (snowy wood-rush). The latter has clusters of tiny, white flowers, which speckle the quartet from above, like flits of light.

Happy in dry or damp soil, the hart's tongue fern is useful in what are often considered challenging garden spots, including under a tree, where the dark brown colour of its midribs pick up nicely on the brown colour of the bark. It grows well in dry shade as well as damp, shady soil.

Dryoptris wallichiana is a reliable and adaptable fern suitable for both damp or dry soil and full or partial shade, including the very deep, constant shadow next to a shady wall. In spring, bright green fronds appear anew, taking over from the bottle-green winter foliage. The fronds are widely cut, which gives an illusion of the play of shadow and light, and so adds depth to the garden, as well as giving them their distinctive shuttlecock shape.

You can plant ferns as young plants at any time of year, provided the soil isn't frozen. Water thoroughly on planting and then regularly for the first few weeks, even if it rains.

Goes well with

Hakonechloa macra (Japanese forest grass)
Luzula nivea (snowy wood-rush)

Far left: *Asplenium scolopendrium*

Left: *Asplenium scolopendrium* and *Dryopteris wallichiana*

Latin name	*Astrantia major*
Common name	**greater masterwort**
★	perennial
Plant	early spring to mid-autumn
Flowers	late spring to late summer

height – 60cm (24in)
spacing – 2 per m^2 ($10ft^2$)
soil – any
aspect – sun, partial shade

What appear to be the petals of an astrantia's pincushion-like flower are, in fact, robust, papery bracts, which are wonderfully coloured and resilient to wind and wet weather. The flowers of *Astrantia major*, and to a lesser degree its foliage, have a metallic gleam, which makes this hardy perennial useful in shadow where it bounces back the light. Insects love astrantias – their 'true' flowers are tiny but numerous and packed into their bracts – and are busy with bumblebees, solitary bees and hoverflies in summer.

Goes well with

Dryopteris wallichiana (alpine wood fern)
Hakonechloa macra (Japanese forest grass)
Nepeta 'Six Hills Giant' (catmint)
Thalictrum 'Anne' (meadow rue)

Astrantia major 'Rubra' (masterwort)

Astrantia major 'Florence' (masterwort)

Astrantia major subsp. involucrata 'Shaggy' (masterwort)

Latin name	*Briza media*
Common name	**common quaking grass**
★	short-lived perennial
Plant	early spring to mid-autumn
Flowers	late spring to late summer; colour-changing seedpods follow the flowers in autumn

height – 50cm (20in)
spacing – 4 per m^2 ($10ft^2$)
soil – any
aspect – sun

Briza media is a bright green, clump-forming grass with narrow leaves and delicate flowers that are followed by dangling seedpods. The seedpods start off green with hints of plum, eventually turning silver as summer progresses. It pairs beautifully with *Tulbaghia violacea* (society garlic) and *Eschscholzia californica* 'Ivory Castle' (California poppy), picking up on the plum markings of the tulbaghia's pink flowers and complementing the poppy's creamy-white petals. Its common name, quaking grass, comes from the way the buds and seedpods shimmer and ripple in the breeze.

Goes well with

Eschscholzia californica 'Ivory Castle' (California poppy)
Tulbaghia violacea (society garlic)

Latin name	*Catananche caerulea*
Common name	**Cupid's dart**
★	short-lived perennial
Sow	early to late spring
Plant	early summer
Flowers	early summer to early autumn

height – 70cm (28in)
spacing – 3 per m^2 (10ft^2)
soil – well drained
aspect – sun

Originating from the Mediterranean, *Catananche caerulea* is commonly known as Cupid's dart due to its historical use as an aphrodisiac. This robust and easy-to-grow plant is very pretty and delicate in appearance, with papery, fringed, blue flowers atop wiry stems. Its leaves and stem foliage are a grey-green colour and the flowers have dark purple centres.

Although perennial, *C. caerulea* is very short-lived and better treated as an annual and grown from seed. The seeds are big enough to sow individually, two to a 9cm (3½in) pot, and germinate easily – within one to two weeks. Grow the seedlings indoors, moving them outside after the risk of frost has passed in late spring. It needs plenty of sun.

Goes well with

Achillea 'Terracotta' (yarrow)
Dianthus carthusianorum (carthusian pink)
Eschscholzia californica 'Ivory Castle' (California poppy)
Papaver dubium subsp. *lecoqii* 'Albiflorum' (Beth's poppy)
Verbena bonariensis (purple top)

Latin name	*Cynara cardunculus* AGM
Common name	**cardoon**
★	perennial
Sow	late winter to early spring
Plant	mid-spring to early summer
Flowers	early summer to early autumn

height – 2.4m (8ft)
spacing – 1 per m^2 ($10ft^2$)
soil – any
aspect – sun

As valuable for its foliage as for its flowers, the leaves of cardoon appear early in the year. Grey-green in colour, they are notably different from the typical bright greens of early spring. In a small garden, plants with silver foliage reflect the light, and due to their giant size, cardoons retain this quality even on overcast days. In spring, this perennial is an excellent partner for tulips, echoing the tumbling shapes of their leaves on a large scale and lifting deeper colours. The wedges of light reflected in the leaves are especially useful for drawing attention to the colourful bands of two-tone tulips like *Tulipa* 'Slawa', making their flower colours appear brighter. Plants with silver foliage also create a sense of space, acting as arbitrators between colours that on paper might not seem to work.

Sow two seeds in a pot of seed compost and water carefully. Stand on a warm windowsill, keeping the compost damp. If both seeds germinate, remove the weaker one and leave the other until its roots nearly fill the pot, then transplant into the garden.

Goes well with

Cerinthe major 'Purpurascens'
Lunaria annua 'Corfu Blue' (honesty)
Tulipa 'Gavota'
Tulipa 'Slawa'
Tulipa 'Spring Green'

Latin name	*Dianthus carthusianorum*
Common name	**carthusian pink**
★	perennial
Plant	early spring to mid-autumn
Flowers	mid-summer to early autumn

height – 40cm (16in)
spacing – 2 per m^2 (10ft^2)
soil – any
aspect – sun

Dianthus carthusianorum is a perennial that stands out for its intense pops of colour. The petals of the small, brilliant neon-pink flowers are marked with a darker pink. Its narrow, green foliage is subtle and recedes in comparison to the vibrancy of the flowers, which makes them stand out even more. Yet, despite its brightness, the whole plant has an airy, ethereal quality, with the flowers appearing to hover above the ground, which gives it a sense of lightness and movement.

This perennial pairs well with dahlias that have foliage or flowers in rich colours, such as *Dahlia* 'Waltzing Matilda', as well as with inky *Salvia* 'Nachtvlinder' (sage). For a flash of pink in a scheme that might otherwise feel flat, it is unmatched. The small flowers are also a boon for pollinators like bees and butterflies, drawing them into the garden and boosting biodiversity.

Goes well with

Allium hollandicum 'Purple Sensation' (Dutch garlic)
Dahlia 'Waltzing Mathilda'
Papaver somniferum 'Lauren's Grape' (opium poppy)
Salvia 'Nachtvlinder' (sage)
Verbascum bombyciferum (Broussa mullein)

Latin name	*Digitalis parviflora*
Common name	**small-flowered foxglove**
★	perennial
Plant	early spring to mid-autumn
Flowers	late spring to mid-summer

height – 60cm (24in)
spacing – 1 per m² (10ft²)
soil – any
aspect – partial shade

The nuanced colours of *Digitalis parviflora* make it suitable for many colour combinations. The species name *parviflora* translates from the Latin as 'small flower', and the flowers are indeed small, but plentiful. Its upright habit makes it a light-catcher even though it is shorter and more compact than a traditional foxglove. The toffee-coloured flowers have a velvety quality and shimmer in sunlight.

This foxglove works well with plants that have flowers with pink and purple tones, such as *Salvia* 'Nachtvlinder' (sage) and *Linaria purpurea* 'Canon Went' (purple toadflax), as well as brights like *Euphorbia seguieriana* subsp. *niciciana* (spurge).

In common with all foxgloves, the small-flowered foxglove is also excellent news for pollinators, in particular bees, which enliven its flowers in early summer.

Goes well with

Euphorbia seguieriana subsp. *niciciana* (spurge)
Linaria purpurea 'Canon Went' (purple toadflax)
Salvia 'Nachtvlinder' (sage)

Latin name	*Euphorbia seguieriana* subsp. *niciciana*
Common name	**spurge**
★	perennial
Plant	early to mid-autumn
Flowers	late spring to early autumn

height – 50cm (20in)
spacing – 1 per m^2 ($10ft^2$)
soil – any
aspect – sun

Euphorbias embody brightness, standing out among the more muted greens and greys typical of plants that like sun. *Euphorbia seguieriana* subsp. *niciciana* makes a neat, rounded mound that sits easily in a small outdoor space and works best when given enough room to demonstrate its natural habit. With electric-green foliage and yellow flower bracts, it is also a useful anchor for more off-beat colours, such as burnt-orange and toffee, as well as providing a good foil for brighter tones. This spurge works particularly well with annual poppies, *Cerinthe major* 'Purpurascens' (honeywort) and *Catananche caerulea* (Cupid's dart).

Goes well with

Catananche caerulea (Cupid's dart)
Cerinthe major 'Purpurascens' (honeywort)
Linaria purpurea 'Canon Went' (purple toadflax)
Sanguisorba officinalis 'Arnhem' (great burnet)

Latin name	*Geranium* Rozanne ('Gerwat') AGM
Common name	**cranesbill**
★	perennial
Plant	early spring to mid-autumn
Flowers	late spring to mid-autumn

height – 60cm (24in)
spacing – 2 per m² (10ft²)
soil – any
aspect – partial shade

People often refer to the brightly coloured flowers that are usually grown in terracotta pots on windowsills as 'geraniums', but these are, in fact, pelargoniums. True geraniums are bigger plants with plentiful round flowers that can survive winter outdoors.

The violet-blue flowers of *Geranium* Rozanne ('Gerwat') have white centres. Useful in shade, it is an excellent partner for ferns in a sunken courtyard or a side return. Alternatively, it works well with blue-flowered *Nepeta racemosa* 'Walker's Low' (catmint). In autumn, the leaves take on warm red tones.

Goes well with

Asplenium scolopendrium (hart's tongue fern)
Dryopteris (wood fern)
Nepeta racemosa 'Walker's Low' (catmint)
Nepeta 'Six Hills Giant' (catmint)

Latin name	*Geum* 'Lemon Drops'
Common name	**avens**
★	perennial
Plant	early spring to mid-autumn
Flowers	late spring to mid-summer

height – 40cm (16in)
spacing – 2 per m^2 ($10ft^2$)
soil – any
aspect – sun

Geum 'Lemon Drops' has small, yellow flowers that appear to hover on their narrow, gently curving stems. The flowers nod downwards and have a hint of green in their petals, which gives this plant a slightly woodsy and nicely wild appearance, making it easy to use in a contemporary garden. The flowers open in swift succession and are also easily accessible, which makes this perennial a popular choice for pollinators. The flowers often have a slightly ruffled look that adds texture to the garden.

G. 'Lemon Drops' makes a pretty and subtle pairing with *Lunaria annua* 'Corfu Blue' (honesty), which picks up on the pink hue of the outer petals. It makes an excellent selection for the edge of a path, as it is easily lost in the middle of a border.

Goes well with

Allium siculum (Sicilian honey garlic)
Lunaria annua 'Corfu Blue' (honesty)
Tulipa 'Spring Green' (tulip)

Latin name	*Hakonechloa macra* AGM
Common name	**Japanese forest grass**
★	perennial
Plant	late spring to late autumn
Flowers	early to mid-summer (although usually grown for its foliage); delicate seedpods follow the flowers

height – 30cm (12in)
spacing – 3 per m^2 ($10ft^2$)
soil – any
aspect – sun or partial shade

This clump-forming grass has chunky, narrow leaves, which are a bright chartreuse-green on emerging, browning to papery tones in early winter. The leaves spill out and down under their own weight and are accompanied by lime-green seedpods, which turn towards brown as summer progresses. It is a good companion for ferns, adding texture and brightness at a similar height among their unfurling, dark green-brown croziers and contributing to their myriad greens later. This fern-forest grass combination works well speckled with every colour of tulip, the tonal greens throwing them into pretty relief. Later, after the bulbs finish flowering, their foliage is easily lost among the other leaves.

This grass can be slow to start growing but is well worth the wait, as it never overwhelms its planting spot and makes a year-round contribution. As with all low, clumping grasses, repetition is key. Plant at least three to make a group, arranging them irregularly. Being perennial, new green shoots push up each spring – the cue to cut off last year's brown foliage.

Goes well with

Asplenium scolopendrium (hart's-tongue fern)
Dryopteris (wood fern)
Luzula nivea grass (snowy wood-rush)
Tulipa (tulip)

Latin name	*Melica altissima* 'Alba'
Common name	**Siberian melic**
★	perennial
Plant	early spring to mid-autumn
Flowers	mid-spring to early summer, but typically grown for its foliage

height – 60cm (24in)
spacing – 3 per m^2 ($10ft^2$)
soil – any
aspect – any

Melica altissima 'Alba' is a low, hummock-forming grass that is understated enough to use with a wide range of different plants. Its narrow leaves are a bright shade of green and knit easily together to create a meadow-like effect that elevates both bold and subtle colours in the garden.

In early summer, minuscule, gleaming, white flowers hover proud of the grassy foliage and are later followed by equally tiny seeds, resembling grains of rice and arranged as ethereal seedheads. Both the flowers and seedheads have a subtle shimmer and reflect the light beautifully. Siberian melic pairs particularly well with *Allium* 'Millennium' (ornamental onion), which leans towards pink, creating a harmonious contrast.

This grass grows as well in a container as it does in the open garden, making it a go-to plant for a wide range of planting schemes.

Goes well with

Allium 'Millennium' (ornamental onion)
Allium siculum (Sicilian honey garlic)
Salvia 'Nachtvlinder' (sage)

Latin name	*Nepeta racemosa* 'Walker's Low' AGM
Common name	**catmint**
★	perennial
Plant	early spring to mid-autumn
Flowers	early summer to early autumn

height – 60cm (24in)
spacing – 3 per m^2 ($10ft^2$)
soil – any
aspect – partial shade, sun

Crush the leaves of *Nepeta racemosa* 'Walker's Low' between your fingers and it releases the scent of lemon and spice. Its tiny trumpet flowers are a vivid, almost iridescent blue and held above chalky green foliage. It is quite a lax plant with a tendency to flop over but will happily survive the odd flip-flop or boot if it is planted at the edge of a path, which makes it release its wonderful fragrance.

The blue flowers and green leaves complement other chalky plant tones, and it is also very long-flowering. Each of the small trumpet flowers has a protruding lip, which acts like a landing pad for pollinators, encouraging them into the flowers and, being bee-blue, it is very popular with bees in particular.

Taller and hardier is the catmint *N.* 'Six Hills Giant', which will prove useful if you are gardening in colder climates.

Goes well with

Achillea 'Terracotta' (yarrow)
Salvia 'Nachtvlinder' (sage)

Latin name	*Papaver rupifragum*
Common name	**Spanish poppy**
★	perennial
Plant	early spring to mid-autumn
Flowers	early to late summer; decorative seedheads follow the flowers

height – 40cm (16in)
spacing – 1 per m^2 ($10ft^2$)
soil – any
aspect – sun

Despite its delicate appearance, the poppy *Papaver rupifragum* flowers for many months and returns reliably every year. It pairs beautifully with plants with sharp colours that draw out the brightness of its flowers, such as *Euphorbia* (spurge), and also with those that have similarly meadow-esque qualities, like *Orlaya grandiflora* (white laceflower).

With new flowers opening daily during summer, *P. rupifragum* makes an excellent choice for containers. After the petals drop, the flowers are replaced by lovely decorative seedheads, which turn grey and papery in the autumn.

Goes well with

Euphorbia (spurge)
Orlaya grandiflora (white laceflower)

Latin name	*Pulsatilla vulgaris* AGM
Common name	**pasqueflower**
★	perennial
Plant	early spring to early autumn
Flowers	mid- to late spring; fluffy seedheads follow the flowers

height – 20cm (8in)
spacing – 3 per m^2 ($10ft^2$)
soil – well drained
aspect – sun

Pulsatilla vulgaris makes a pretty, low detail where it can benefit from the warmth of the sun, although it will open its blooms whatever the weather. The small, violet, bell-shaped flowers tilt upwards as they open, revealing a yellow, stamen-filled centre. The flowers are held in a green ruff of filigree fronds, while above the feathery, green foliage, the buds, flowers and stems have long, silky hairs that give the plant a silvery appearance.

This perennial works best grown with plants that bring out its purple hues, such as the dark and light, two-tone flowers of *Linaria maroccana* 'Licilia Violet' (Moroccan toadflax) and rich purple *Salvia* 'Nachtvlinder' (sage). The pale, creamy flowers of *Eschscholzia californica* 'Ivory Castle' (California poppy) are another good match, echoing the silvery quality of the pulsatilla's mother-of-pearl-esque flowers. Both grow to a similar size and at a similar rate. In a small garden, this combination is lovely alongside the tiny-leaved, silver-green *Thymus* 'Fragrantissimus' (orange-scented thyme).

From late spring, the flowers morph into fluffy, green seedheads with a pinkish hue. Despite their fragile appearance, they are fairly robust and will last for months outside. Later in summer, *Tulbaghia violacea* (society garlic) will emulate their hovering habit and echo their colour in a different hue.

After planting, this perennial can be slow to flower, but it is worth the wait for the year-round contribution it makes to the garden. It is also a popular plant with pollinators.

Goes well with

Eschscholzia californica 'Ivory Castle' (California poppy)
Linaria maroccana 'Licilia Violet' (Moroccan toadflax)
Papaver commutatum 'Ladybird' (poppy)
Papaver dubium subsp. *lecoqii* 'Albiflorum' (Beth's poppy)
Salvia 'Nachtvlinder' (sage)
Thymus 'Fragrantissimus' (orange-scented thyme)
Tulbaghia violacea (society garlic)

Pulsatilla vulgaris in flower and the delicate seedheads that follow.

Latin name	*Rosa* × *odorata* 'Mutabilis' AGM
Common name	**tea rose**
★	perennial
Plant	early spring to mid-autumn
Flowers	late spring to late autumn

height – 2.4m (8ft)
spacing – 1 per m^2 (10ft^2)
soil – any
aspect – sun

Due to the simple shape of its flowers, *Rosa* × *odorata* 'Mutabilis' is very much in vogue. The cultivar name 'Mutabilis' translates from the Latin as 'changing', and the flowers, which appear on shoots that are bronze in spring, are valuable for their shifting colours. They start yellow and then turn rich pink, before eventually reaching crimson.

The flowers appear intermittently from spring until autumn and are a good match for every type of plant, from tulips to asters. Unlike highly bred roses that are often densely packed with petals, the open flowers of this tea rose are useful for pollinators.

Goes well with

Euphorbia seguieriana subsp. *niciciana* (spurge)
Tulipa 'Gavota' (tulip)
Tulipa 'Slawa' (tulip)

Latin name	*Salvia* 'Nachtvlinder' AGM
Common name	**sage**
★	perennial
Plant	early spring to mid-autumn
Flowers	late spring to late autumn

height – 60cm (24in)
spacing – 1 per m^2 (10ft^2)
soil – well drained
aspect – sun

Salvia 'Nachtvlinder' is a versatile plant with rich violet flowers. The intensity of its petal colour leans towards black, while the narrow stems and small, sparse leaves give it a transparent quality. As a consequence, the flowers register against themselves, as much as other plants. The cultivar name 'Nachtvlinder' translates from the Dutch as 'night moth', which alludes to its dark, moody colour. The rich, dark hues of the flowers makes them stand out against garden foliage, especially in bright sunlight. Note that it needs a lot of light to show its true colour.

This perennial pairs beautifully with *Cerinthe major* 'Purpurascens' (honeywort), the dark hues of the salvia enhancing the cerinthe's muted, metallic blue tones. It is also a good match for alliums in lighter and darker shades of purple.

Originating from the Mediterranean, sage is adapted to hot, dry conditions and, as our weather patterns shift as a consequence of climate change, makes an ideal choice for sustainable gardening. Its flowers draw a wide range of pollinators throughout the summer.

Goes well with

Cerinthe major 'Purpurascens' (honeywort)
Nepeta racemosa 'Walkers Low' (catmint)
Verbena officinalis 'Bampton' (vervain)

Latin name	*Salvia nemorosa* 'Caradonna' AGM
Common name	**Balkan clary**
★	perennial
Plant	early spring to mid-autumn
Flowers	early summer to mid-autumn

height – 60cm (24in)
spacing – 2 per m^2 ($10ft^2$)
soil – any
aspect – sun

Very much the garden designers' favourite salvia, *Salvia nemorosa* 'Caradonna' stands out for the darkness of its stems and the indigo flowers. Even before the flowers open in summer, darkly crossed buds hold their own in the early light.

It is a good companion for *Nepeta racemosa* 'Walker's Low' (catmint), which has blue flowers and reaches a similar height, and can provide a useful understorey for spring bulbs, which flower in the space above it.

Goes well with

Allium hollandicum 'Purple Sensation' (Dutch garlic)
Allium siculum (Sicilian honey garlic)
Dianthus carthusianorum (carthusian pink)
Nepeta racemosa 'Walker's Low' (catmint)

Latin name	*Salvia officinalis* 'Purpurascens' AGM
Common name	**purple sage**
★	woody perennial
Plant	early spring to mid-autumn
Flowers	late spring to mid-summer (although usually grown for its striking foliage)

height – 50cm (20in)
spacing – 1 per m^2 ($10ft^2$)
soil – well-drained
aspect – sun

Salvia officinalis 'Purpurascens' is best known as the edible herb sage. With felty leaves in various shades of plum and green, it absorbs the light and provides a useful counterpoint to taller and airier plants. It makes a low hump in the ground and pairs beautifully with *Verbena officinalis* 'Bampton' (vervain), offering a contrast in both colour and density. The velvety, plum-toned leaves of the sage provide a rich, tactile backdrop that highlights the verbena's delicate and semi-transparent nature. It is also lovely paired with *Cerinthe major* 'Purpurascens' (honeywort), highlighting the dusky blue of the flowers and the tips of the leaves.

Salvia officinalis 'Purpurascens' turns more deeply purple in the heat of the sun, becoming greener in the shade. It is an evergreen perennial, and so maintains a constant presence in the garden.

Sage can be grown in containers, which is ideal in small spaces and for bringing the herb closer to the kitchen for easy picking.

Goes well with

Cerinthe major 'Purpurascens' (honeywort)
Linaria maroccana 'Licilia Violet' (Moroccan toadflax)
Verbena officinalis 'Bampton' (vervain)

Latin name	*Salvia rosmarinus*
Common name	**rosemary**
★	woody perennial
Plant	early spring to mid-autumn
Flowers	mid-spring to late summer

height – 30–60cm (12-24in)
spacing – 1 per m² (10ft²)
soil – well drained
aspect – sun

Plants with evergreen foliage make good anchors around which to combine both early- and late-flowering plants. Rosemary is a woody shrub with a wonderfully graphic outline which is created by the needle-fine foliage. The depth of the green of its leaves is leavened by their narrowness, making it a useful foil for a wide range of plants.

There are many varieties of rosemary – some are tall and narrow and others low and flat. *Salvia rosmarinus* 'Miss Jessop's Upright' is a tall variety with tiny, brilliant blue flowers and a greenish-blue tint to the foliage. It pairs well with blue and purple flowers, such as those of 'Nachtvlinder' (sage) and *Cerinthe major* 'Purpurascens' (honeywort). *Salvia r.* 'Prostratus Group' is a low, horizontal form that makes a good choice for gravel gardens, or those planted in builder's rubble, among shorter plants such as *Pulsatilla vulgaris* (pasque flowers).

All varieties of rosemary are edible. Position in a spot where the plant will benefit from the warmth of the sun to heighten its resinous scent.

Goes well with

Cerinthe major 'Purpurascens' (honeywort)
Linaria maroccana 'Licilia violet' (Moroccan toadflax)
Pulsatilla vulgaris (pasque flower)
Salvia 'Nachtvlinder' (sage)

Latin name	*Sanguisorba officinalis* 'Arnhem'
Common name	**great burnet**
★	perennial
Plant	early spring to mid-autumn
Flowers	early to late summer

height – 2m (6½ft)
spacing – 2 per m² (10ft²)
soil – any
aspect – sun, partial shade

With crimson, button-like flowers that open in unison, *Sanguisorba officinalis* 'Arnhem' provides a continuum of colour. The flowers sit atop tall, narrow stems, which can reach up to 2m (6½ft) in height. Tall plants with quasi-transparent qualities like this are very useful for obscuring sightlines in a small space, allowing a glimpse of what lies beyond. It flowers during summer when the light is at its most intense, which further saturates the red colour of its flowers.

Goes well with

Euphorbia seguieriana subsp. *niciciana* (spurge)
Linaria maroccana 'Licilia Violet' (Moroccan toadflax)
Thalictrum 'Elin' (meadow rue)

Latin name	*Symphyotrichum* 'Little Carlow' AGM
Common name	**aster, Michaelmas daisy**
★	perennial
Plant	early spring to mid-autumn
Flowers	late summer to mid-autumn

height – 90cm (36in)
spacing – 2 per m² (10ft²)
soil – any
aspect – sun, partial shade

Symphyotrichum 'Little Carlow' is a dainty but voluminous plant with small, daisy-like flowers that are dotted in the centre with a bright yellow eye. It is one of the first flowers of autumn and useful for extending the colour interest in a small garden. The flowers retain their colour, even as those of other plants are fading around them, and are a magnet for late-flying pollinators.

The lilac petals draw out the pinkish hues of allium seedheads, and it is also a good match for the windflower *Anemone* Wild Swan ('Macane001'), which shares the same yellow in the centre of its flowers.

Tiny leaves and dark, narrow stems give this perennial a transparent quality and it does well in places that are in shadow for much of the day, lifting the shade with its colours.

Goes well with

Allium hollandicum 'Purple Sensation'
Anemone Wild Swan ('Macane001') (windflower)

Latin name	*Thalictrum* 'Elin' AGM
Common name	**meadow rue**
★	perennial
Plant	early spring to mid-autumn
Flowers	early to late summer

height – 2m (6½ft)
spacing – 1 per m^2 ($10ft^2$)
soil – any
aspect – sun, partial shade

The hundreds of tiny flowers of thalictrum register together to create a haze of colour, up to 2m (6½ft) high. In both bud and flower, *Thalictrum* 'Elin' is a plant with shimmering qualities that work well with other silvery plants.

The dark foliage is arranged horizontally, in widely spaced layers, making it a useful plant for adding height without casting too much shadow in a small outdoor space, much as a light-limbed tree might.

The colour of the foliage makes it a good match for plants with dark-coloured flowers, such as *Salvia* 'Nachtvlinder' (sage) and *Linaria maroccana* 'Licilia Violet' (Moroccan toadflax). It also works well with pink, which brings out its grey tones.

Goes well with

Astrantia major subsp. *involucrata* 'Shaggy' (masterwort)
Linaria maroccana 'Licilia Violet' (Moroccan toadflax)
Salvia 'Nachtvlinder' (sage)
Verbascum bombyciferum (Broussa mullein)

The airy, white flowers and pretty, purple-tinged leaves and stems of *Thalictrum* 'Elin'

Latin name	*Thymus* 'Fragrantissimus' AGM
Common name	**orange-scented thyme**
★	woody perennial
Plant	early spring to mid-autumn
Flowers	early to late summer

height – 20cm (8in)
spacing – 1 per m^2 (10ft^2)
soil – well drained, sandy
aspect – sun

A ground-hugging, evergreen perennial with small, fragrant leaves and tiny, white flowers in summer, woody *Thymus* 'Fragrantissimus' contributes to the balance of heights and shapes in a small garden and is good company for a wide range of plants. It makes a pretty detail at low level, evoking a sense of a wild, unmanaged space, and so sits easily among plants with simple, single flowers, while maintaining a sense of design. Its small flowers and leaves mean it is visually complex despite its diminutive size.

Thyme provides a textural contrast with taller, more upright plants, allowing light to drop between them, almost to ground level in places.

The ability of thyme to thrive in hungry, well-drained soils, with little water, makes it a hardy and fuss-free option. The grey-green leaves of *T.* 'Fragrantissimus' emit a lovely fragrance of balsam and oranges, while the pink flowers are appealing to bees and other pollinators.

Goes well with

Eschscholzia californica 'Ivory Castle' (California poppy)
Pulsatilla vulgaris (pasque flower)
Thalictrum 'Elin' (meadow rue)

Latin name	*Tulbaghia violacea*
Common name	**society garlic**
★	perennial
Plant	early spring to mid-autumn
Flowers	early summer to late autumn

height – 50cm (20in)
spacing – 1 per m^2 ($10ft^2$)
soil – well drained
aspect – sun

Tulbaghia violacea is a refreshing blend of beauty and reliability. Its grass-like leaves provide a subtle backdrop for umbels of star-like flowers, gently recurved at their tips, and it flowers non-stop from early summer until the end of autumn. The dainty flowers are made up of trumpets that radiate from a central point at the top of each stem. Since the foliage is narrow and recessive, it is almost invisible compared to the flowers and so these appear to hover, as if suspended. The pink tone of the flowers is at the violet end of the spectrum, and so this perennial is at its best at the start and end of the day when it looks luminous in the half-light. It is a magnet for small pollinators like bees and hoverflies, which animate its flowers.

In a small garden, siting this perennial needs careful thought, as the space created by the stems between the base and the flowers is lost if it is too close to other plants. It pairs well with other sun-lovers like *Linaria* (honesty) and *Cerinthe major* 'Purpurascens' (honeywort), the scale of whose flowers echo its delicacy, creating a pretty, layered combination.

Goes well with

Cerinthe major 'Purpurascens' (honeywort)
Dianthus carthusianorum (carthusian pink)
Erigeron karvinskianus (Mexican fleabane)
Gladiolus papilio (butterfly sword lily)
Linaria (honesty)
Papaver dubium subsp. *lecoqii* 'Albiflorum' (Beth's poppy)
Papaver somniferum (opium poppy)

Latin name	*Verbena officinalis* 'Bampton'
Common name	**vervain**
★	perennial
Plant	early spring to mid-autumn
Flowers	early summer to early autumn

height – 1m (39in)
spacing – 1 per m^2 ($10ft^2$)
soil – any
aspect – sun

The liquorice-coloured foliage of *Verbena officinalis* 'Bampton' has an iridescent sheen, which adds depth to the fresh, bright greens of early summer. Its many small, bright lilac-pink flowers are held at the tips of a scaffold of dark, narrow stems. The small size of the flowers and their airy distribution create a light, ethereal effect, and the flowers, which appear at the same time, register together to create a wash of colour.

This perennial pairs well with plants that have green or chalky foliage and fresh, vibrantly coloured flowers. Consider combining it with the yellow-flowered *Verbascum bombyciferum* 'Polarsommer' (mullein) or glaucous blue *Cerinthe major* 'Purpurascens' (honeywort).

This verbena is notable for being super long-flowering and the tiny, densely packed flowers are not only pretty but also brilliant at providing nectar – for smaller pollinators in particular.

Goes well with

Cerinthe major 'Purpurascens' (honeywort)
Salvia 'Nachtvlinder' (sage)
Verbascum bombyciferum 'Polarsommer' (mullein)

Bulbs

True bulbs, corms, tubers and rhizomes all come under the umbrella term 'bulb'. They are dormant, underground stems, leaves and roots, often wrapped in a dry, papery packaging, which are ready to grow as soon as environmental conditions become favourable. Bulbs contain almost everything they need to flower.

- Key to success with bulbs is planting them at the right time. Spring-flowering bulbs, such tulips and alliums, should be planted in autumn, so they can spend winter underground in the cold and dark. Summer-flowering bulbs, such as dahlias, need to be planted in springtime.

- Bulbs are hard to beat for exaggerating the changing of the seasons, drawing our attention outside. Although spring usually comes to mind when we think about bulbs, lots of bulbs flower at a different time of year.

- Choosing which bulbs to plant is very enjoyable, as they are available in a huge range of colours and shapes with plenty of choice to fit any planting scheme. There are also bulbs for every soil and situation. There is something appealing about choosing spring-flowering bulbs in autumn and knowing during the dark days of winter that they are outside waiting for the arrival of spring.

- Bulbs that flower early or late in the year are particularly useful for pollinators, offering foraging opportunities at times when these are in short supply.

- Although, traditionally, bulbs have had poor environmental credentials due to their throwaway nature, the chemicals and amount of water used in their commercial production, and the costs involved in their overseas transport, in the UK a shift towards bulbs that are perennial, British-grown and chemical-free means they now have a positive environmental impact, sequestering carbon and widening the diversity of pollinators.

Latin name	*Allium*
Common name	**ornamental onion**
★	bulb
Plant	mid- to late autumn
Flowers	late spring to late summer; the architectural seedheads that follow the flowers last into winter

height – 40–90cm (16–36in)
spacing – 5–10 per m² (10ft²)
soil – well drained
aspect – full sun

Alliums, with their near-round flowers, win top prize for their bold colours and long-lasting, architectural shapes. Held one flower per stem at mid-height, each bloom is made up of hundreds of tiny florets arranged in orbit around a single, central point. The flowers appear to hover on account of their straight, upright stems and low, narrow foliage, offering plenty of room below for other plants. The flowers are available on a sliding scale of purple shades, from lilac to blackcurrant, and there is an allium suitable for any scheme or garden situation.

Post-bloom, bobbled seedheads repeat the shapes of the original flowers, taking on hues of brown and milky white. These seedheads are beautifully graphic and very robust, straddling the seasons and continuing to decorate the garden through the winter months.

Allium hollandicum 'Purple Sensation' (Dutch garlic) has true purple flowers that look beautiful with both lighter and darker purple flowers, stems and foliage. The flowers are held atop stems that are resolutely upright and pair well with plants on more relaxed stems, such as *Geum* (avens) and *Papaver* (poppy), which draw out the alliums' wilder qualities, as well as accentuating the hints of plum and black in their flowers.

The ornamental onion *A.* 'Millennium', which leans towards pink, looks lovely alongside low, clumping grasses like *Melica altissima* 'Alba' (Siberian melic), whose tiny, white flowers similarly ping back the light.

The small, round flowers of *A. sphaerocephalon* (drumstick allium) start green and blend with surrounding greenery until their blackcurrant hue emerges in summer.

Goes well with

Lunaria annua 'Corfu Blue' (honesty)
Melica altissima 'Alba' (Siberian melic)
Papaver commutatum 'Ladybird' (poppy)
Salvia 'Nachtvlinder' (sage)
Tulipa 'Spring Green' (tulip)

Allium hollandicum 'Purple Sensation' (Dutch garlic)

Allium 'Millennium' (ornamental onion)

Allium sphaerocephalon (drumstick allium)

Deserving a special mention is *A. siculum* (Sicilian honey garlic). This pendulous allium with captivating flowers is characterized by pale pink and white stripes and a greenish-grey tinge. The flowers are held on gently arching stems and appear to hover, giving the plant a natural, somewhat wild, appearance that integrates effortlessly into contemporary gardens. Its pale colours are especially effective at brightening up shady spots, making it an ideal choice for adding lightness to partially shaded areas, where it thrives. *Allium siculum* works beautifully with green-flashed *Tulipa* 'Spring Green', the tulip's tinged petals resonating with the allium's iridescent stripes to make an intriguing combination. Both plants are reliably perennial and flower simultaneously.

Allium flowers are brimful of pollen and nectar, which makes them very popular with pollinators. In fact, *Nectaroscordum*, the synonym of the *Allium* genus, refers to its nectar-rich flowers, with *A. siculum* in particular being a very popular flowering bulb with pollinators. After the flowers have been pollinated, their individual florets turn sharply upwards, like the turrets of a castle, taking on muted colours.

In autumn, plant allium bulbs 15cm (6in) deep, in groups of up to ten, spacing them irregularly. Leave enough room between individual bulbs to avoid overcrowding the flowers when they open.

The dangling, stripy flowers of *Allium siculum* are popular with bees and turn upwards after they have been pollinated.

Latin name	*Dahlia*
Common name	**dahlia**
★	tuber
Plant	late spring to early summer
Flowers	mid-summer to late autumn

height – 70cm–1.5m (28in–5ft)
spacing – 1 per m^2 ($10ft^2$)
soil – well drained
aspect – sun

Dahlias have eight sets of chromosomes, whereas most plants have just two, resulting in a remarkable variety of flower colours and shapes. This genetic variety also offers limitless possibilities for plant breeders in search of something new and explains the extensive range of dahlias available. Their wide and nuanced colour spectrum, with its varying hues and intensities, makes them particularly versatile for colourful and contemporary combinations. Some cultivars have the additional bonus of dark crimson-brown foliage and stems, which add depth to their richly coloured flowers and throw paler flowers into pretty relief.

'Single' dahlias have a single row of petals and an open centre with a plentiful supply of pollen and nectar, which makes them the most beneficial to pollinators. The simple flowers are also closer to the flower forms found in nature, so they mix with other plants without jarring and are the easiest to use in a small outdoor space.

Easy-going *Dahlia merckii* (Merck dahlia) is a wonderful species that has fresh pink flowers with a muted yellow centre. Supported atop tall, narrow stems, the flowers nod gently, allowing sunlight to reach the plants below during the second half of summer. *Dahlia* 'Twynings After Eight' has creamy, vanilla flowers with a smudge of yellow at the base of the petals, burnt orange centres and bright orange anthers. Rich brown foliage adds an extra layer of colour. *Dahlia*'Roxy' has relatively small flowers, which makes it an excellent choice for containers. Neon-pink petals and brown-red centres mean it pairs well with darker colours.

Goes well with

Dianthus carthusianorum (carthusian pink)
Salvia 'Amistad' (sage)

Dahlia merckii

Dahlia Happy Single Wink ('HS Wink')

Dahlia 'Mary Eveline'

For containers, *D.* 'Bishop of Auckland' is another short variety with dark red, single flowers and even darker, green foliage. *Dahlia* 'Waltzing Matilda', with its apricot-orange blooms marked with deeper orange edges and a slight twist, is a popular contemporary choice. Despite having semi-double flowers, these are open at the centre. 'Waltzing Matilda' pairs well with *Dianthus carthusianorum* (carthusian pink), creating a colourful and long-flowering duo.

Native to Mexico and Central America, Dahlias have traditionally not been considered hardy in the UK climate but, as a result of changing weather patterns and new milder winters, most dahlias will now survive outdoors in all but the coldest, wettest winter. The first of the frost in late autumn will blacken their foliage and they will stop flowering for the year, but the tuber will survive to flower again the following summer. If you experience harsh winters, lift and store the tubers in a frost-free place over winter or use an insulating mulch.

Dahlias can be purchased as potted plants in early summer, but they are very easy and less expensive to grow from dormant tubers planted in late spring, which has the benefit of offering a much wider choice of interesting cultivars.

Start with a firm, healthy tuber – dormant, it will look like bunches of fat, brown carrots dangling from a central point, which is the base of the previous year's flowering stem. Plant each tuber in early spring in a big container of general-purpose compost, to a depth of 15cm (6in). Water once on planting and keep the container on a warm, sunny windowsill. As the first shoots appear, start watering regularly, keeping the compost just damp. Plant outside towards the end of late spring, after all risk of frost has passed.

Alternatively, in early summer you can plant tubers straight outside, to flower a little later.

Dahlia 'Twynings After Eight'

Dahlia 'Waltzing Matilda' with *Dianthus carthusianorum*

Latin name	*Gladiolus papilio*
Common name	**butterfly sword lily**
★	corm
Plant	late spring to early summer
Flowers	mid- to late summer

height – 75cm (30in)
spacing – 1 per m^2 ($10ft^2$)
soil – well drained, sandy
aspect – sun

Matching intense colour with a simple outline, *Gladiolus papilio* is hard to beat for poise and grace. Unlike traditional gladioli, which have been bred to be as densely flowered as possible, its blooms are simple and widely spaced on gently arching stems. The lilac petals are tinged with yellow at their tips and have a deeper yellow flash accented by a dark plum blotch inside, offering plenty of inspiration for creating colourful planting combinations. Flat, upright foliage makes this gladiolus easy to combine with other plants. For example, it beautifully complements *Tulbaghia violacea* (society garlic), which has flowers at the violet end of pink. And it is lovely among low grasses like *Melica altissima* 'Alba' (Siberian melic), its flowers opening in the empty space above them.

Even though the blooms do not open widely, they are a magnet for bees and other pollinators that are flying during summer.

Plant corms at a depth of 15cm (6in) in general-purpose compost in late spring, as this plant does not tolerate frost. You can also start *G. papilio* off earlier in pots, if you protect it from cold weather.

Goes well with

Melica altissima 'Alba' (Siberian melic)
Tulbaghia violacea (society garlic)

Latin name	*Narcissus*
Common name	**daffodil**
★	bulb
Plant	autumn
Flowers	early to mid-spring

height – 30cm (12in)
spacing – 10–15 per m² (10ft²)
soil – any
aspect – sun or partial shade

The emergence of daffodils is a sure sign that spring is on its way. As well as the familiar yellow flowers, there are many other daffodils in varying sizes, heights and colours. This means they lend themselves well to being used in different ways. It is also worth looking at the heft of a daffodil's foliage – using varieties with narrower leaves means the spent foliage is more easily lost post-flower among plants that flower later.

At the muted end of the spectrum, sweet-scented, white-flowered *Narcissus* 'Thalia' is useful for illuminating shade. Another favourite is *N. poeticus* var. *recurvus*, known commonly as old pheasant's eye, which has white flowers with an orange-yellow cup and a burnt orange rim.

In the garden, plant bulbs 15cm (6in) deep in autumn, in groups of 10–15 bulbs, spacing them irregularly. For a pot, a useful rule of thumb is to match the number of bulbs per pot to the width of the pot in centimetres. For instance, plant 20 bulbs if the pot is 20cm (8in) wide. After flowering, use your fingers to snap off the seedpods to redirect energy underground and replenish resources for the following year.

Goes well with

Tulipa 'Ballerina' (tulip)
Tulipa 'Estrella Rijnveld' (tulip)

Narcissus 'Thalia' is the best and perhaps the most beautiful of the pale daffodils and will also grow happily in a container. Planting a handful of bulbs in a windowbox or tabletop tub with acid-yellow *Euphorbia amygdaloides* 'Purpurea' (wood spurge) will provide a burst of spring colour.

Latin name	*Tulipa*
Common name	**tulip**
★	bulb
Plant	mid- to late autumn
Flowers	mid- to late spring

height – 40cm (16in)
spacing – 10–15 per m^2 (10ft^2)
soil – any
aspect – any

Tulips are available in a vast and wonderful array of colours, from rich and saturated, to bold and bright, to subtle and pale. The range of colours is very nuanced, which makes tulips invaluable for creating clever planting combinations. In addition, they flower early in the year, at a time when there are few other colours about to compete.

In a small space, it is best to limit the palette of tulips to three to five different colours that will chime with or offset each other. Otherwise, it is simply a case of choosing the colours that you like.

Straightforward and very reliable, tulips are one of the best candidates for growing in containers. A pot of a single, repeating cultivar works well. Alternatively, choose two different cultivars with common colours, then add up to three more in lighter and darker hues for subtlety and depth.

Over 300 million tulip bulbs are imported into the UK from Holland every year, and while most tulips flower only once, just as we have seen with fast fashion and single-use plastics, their disposable nature can

Goes well with

Cynara cardunculus (cardoon)
Lunaria annua 'Corfu Blue' (honesty)
Narcissus poeticus var. *recurvus* (old pheasant's eye)

Left: The bulbs used in containers can be changed every year, offering scope for creative combinations.

Below: Viridiflora tulips are recognizable due to the green beam that runs down the middle of each petal. *Tulipa* 'Spring Green' is a reliable perennial tulip with white petals marked with green. Its flowers are narrow and pointed at the tips, with echoes of a wild flower.

mean a high carbon footprint in terms of the water needed to produce them commercially and the fossil fuels used in their transport. A more sustainable approach is to choose tulip varieties that are reliably perennial and plant them once where they will come back every spring. While all the energy in a tulip bulb is used up when it flowers, in some types of tulip, new small bulbs (called offsets) appear next to the original bulb when it flowers, and these can grow big enough to flower themselves the following year.

Botanically, tulips are split into 16 groups and it is thought perennial tulips fall into the Viridiflora, Triumph and Parrot groups. They also include species tulips like *Tulipa sylvestris* (wild tulip). In Viridiflora tulips, such as *T.* 'Spring Green', current thinking is that the presence of green in the petals, as well as the leaves and stem, allows the plant to produce more energy through photosynthesis to bulk up the new, young bulb.

In autumn, plant bulbs 15cm (6in) deep in groups or clusters of 10–15, spacing them irregularly and with the occasional outlier, to emulate the patterns they make in nature. Keep like-colours-with-like rather than mixing the colours. Tulips work well among the emergent foliage of summer-flowering perennials, where their spent foliage is easily lost after they have flowered. Post-flower, use your fingers to snap off the seedpods to redirect energy back into the bulb underground.

In a container, plant bulbs 15cm (6in) deep in general-purpose compost and space a finger's-width apart. A handful of horticultural grit under each bulb is helpful for increasing drainage during the mild and wet winters we've been experiencing lately in the UK and to prevent them sitting in wet conditions. Carefully cover the bulbs with more compost and water regularly once shoots appear.

The orange flower of *Tulipa* 'Artist' (Viridiflora Group) is flashed with green in a muted rather than luminous hue, which gives this sumptuous tulip grace and style.

Two-tone tulips such as reliably perennial *Tulipa* 'Slawa' (Triumph Group) are popular for their mesmerizing shades, offering lots of scope for colourful schemes.

The vibrant flowers of *Tulipa* 'Raspberry Ripple' (Triumph Group) are white, swirled with painterly flicks of deep crimson. It makes an excellent cut flower.

A practical colour-by-colour reference guide to help you build your ideal palette.

Colour index

Red

Red encompasses brilliant red and scarlet, crimson, radicchio, raspberry, strawberry, rose, rouge, carmine and Phoenician red. In his book *Chroma: A Book of Colour*, the late filmmaker Derek Jarman wrote that 'No colour is as territorial as red.' It is a colour that works best when used sparingly: in the singular dash of a scarlet poppy or the atomized burst from the deep red flowers of *Sanguisorba officinalis* 'Arnhem' (great burnet).

Red looks wonderful with other strong colours, such as rich purple salvias, in a combination inspired by the inky centres of *Dahlia* 'Bishop's Children' or the black spots on the petals of *Papaver commutatum* 'Ladybird' (poppy), and it provides grounding among sharp, acid brights.

The ability of red to draw attention to itself makes it an excellent choice for using in containers, particularly in small outdoor spaces that are often overlooked, helping to keep the eye within the garden.

Dahlia 'Bishop of Llandaff' (dahlia)

Papaver commutatum 'Ladybird' (poppy)

Sanguisorba officinalis 'Arnhem' (great burnet)

Tulipa 'Jan Reus' (tulip)

Rosa × odorata 'Mutabilis' (tea rose) and *Tulipa* 'Gavota' (tulip)

Astrantia major 'Rubra' (masterwort)

Pink

Pink is quite a flat colour that needs the presence of other colours to draw it out. At the darkest end of its spectrum, planting violet *Salvia* 'Nachtvlinder' (sage) with a stripy, plum-pink allium or the dainty pink umbels of a *Tulbaghia violacea* (society garlic) will highlight their depth and vitality, bringing them to life. Cool, fresh pink is excellent with acid-green and yellow – as seen in the flowers and foliage of *Papaver dubium* subsp. *lecoqii* 'Albiflorum' (Beth's poppy). For a pop of intensity in a group of plants that otherwise lacks vibrancy, wavering neon-pink *Dianthus carthusianorum* (carthusian pink) is hard to beat.

Dahlia merckii (Merck dahlia)

Tulbaghia violacea (society garlic)

Papaver dubium subsp. *lecoqii* 'Albiflorum' (Beth's poppy)

Allium siculum
(Sicilian honey garlic)

Dianthus carthusianorum
(carthusian pink)

Salvia 'Nachtvlinder'
(sage)

Yellow

Ranging from vanilla and butter via sulphur and mustard to sharp, acid-bright, yellow tends to divide opinion more than any other colour.

It makes a pleasing combination with silver, as seen in the yellow flowers and metallic foliage of verbascums or the silver-creaminess of an *Eschscholzia californica* 'Ivory Castle' (California poppy). It also pairs beautifully with green – for example with *Tulipa* 'Spring Green' – and together these hues form a refreshing and versatile backdrop for an array of colours.

At the more vibrant end of the yellow spectrum, its steadying influence is useful for juxtaposing with offbeat colours such as plum, toffee, and coppery bitter orange.

Verbascum bombyciferum (mullein)

Dahlia 'Twynings After Eight' (dahlia)

Euphorbia seguieriana subsp. *niciciana* (spurge)

Tulipa sylvestris
(wild tulip)

Tulipa 'Spring Green'
(tulip)

Euphorbia characias
subsp. *wulfenii*
(Mediterranean spurge)

Geum 'Lemon Drops'
(avens)

Offbeat colours

Bruised colours, such as dusky pink, smoky violet, burnt orange, toffee and milk, are currently in vogue, offering a rich palette of colours that can be used as building blocks for compelling planting schemes. They pair well with almost any colour, including every shade of green. Their versatility stems from their array of nuanced shades, which seamlessly blend with most colours, including different greens.

Gladiolus papilio (butterfly sword lily)

Digitalis parviflora (small-flowered foxglove)

Baptisia 'Dutch Chocolate' (false indigo)

Verbascum 'Petra' (mullein)

White

White is essential for its light-reflecting qualities and ability to elevate other colours. The tiny, white flowers and gleaming seedheads of *Melica altissima* 'Alba' (Siberian melic) are valuable for their ability to ping out and amplify light, making it a favourite plant of garden designers.

White is fresh and zesty, with a sense of the new. Cool whites go well with lime-green and silver, while warm whites are better matched by warmer tones of green.

Many white flowers thrive in shade, and their light-reflecting qualities are invaluable for brightening and transforming darker spaces.

Narcissus poeticus var. *recurvus* (old pheasant's eye)

Melica altissima 'Alba' (Siberian melic)

Orlaya grandiflora (white laceflower)

Symphyotrichum 'Oktoberlicht' (aster)

Silver *Elaeagnus* 'Quicksilver' (oleaster) and *Clematis montana* (Himalayan clematis)

Allium stipitatum 'Everest' (ornamental onion)

Blue

Blues range from sky-blue to cobalt, encompassing tones like modern blue, ultramarine, duck egg and lilac. In nature, blue often has a green or 'glaucous' tint, as seen in the leaves of *Cerinthe major* 'Purpurascens' (honeywort), the colour of which shifts mercurially from green to blue in summer's heat. At the pale end of its spectrum, blue appears luminous and hovering, reverberating in the half-light at the beginning and end of the day, in a similar way to white. A particularly noteworthy shade is 'bee-blue,' a violet-blue hue which is highly attractive to bees and other pollinators drawn to ultraviolet light.

Lunaria annua 'Corfu Blue' (honesty)

Symphyotrichum 'Little Carlow' (aster)

Salvia patens 'Dot's Delight' (gentian sage)

Salvia rosmarinus
(rosemary)

Salvia patens
(gentian sage)

Salvia 'Phyllis Fancy'
(sage)

Deciding whether to grow your plants from seed or buy them is a key part of the creative process when making a garden.

Growing basics

Basic tools

Trowel
A small, sharp trowel is useful for easy planting jobs, including planting bulbs and plants in small pots, saving time and effort. It also doubles up as a scoop for mixing compost and horticultural grit and shovelling compost into every size of container.

Watering can
Choose the biggest you can find, and one with a detachable rose. As well as plants growing in the soil, you can use the detachable rose to water freshly sown seeds and newly germinated seedlings, which require a much gentler jet of water.

Hori hori
This multipurpose, handheld tool is marked with a ruler and has a narrow, double-edged blade for both digging, planting and hoeing off weed seedlings. It is very useful in small or awkward places as well as for planting in soil that contains builder's rubble or is very stony.

Spade
Spades are available in different weights and sizes. A sturdy spade that has been built to last and feels comfortable when you use it is essential for putting in plants that arrive in bigger containers, as well as digging new borders. This is the one piece of equipment I would always recommend buying new, as it's mostly used for fairly heavy-duty tasks.

Plant labels and pencil
Wooden plant labels are inexpensive and 100 per cent recyclable. On labels made of wood, pencil writing stays in place, which isn't the case with a plastic label, and is also legible. You can use and reuse wooden labels, rubbing out and rewriting on them, as well as using both the front and back. Plastic labels end up in landfill.

Plant pots
The plastic pots that come with new plants are a valuable, reusable resource for your own sowing and growing. If buying new, always choose pots made from recyclable materials, such as clay or coir, and then use them repeatedly. Terracotta pots are made from clay that has been quarried from the ground and are recyclable if they break. Black plastic pots cannot be recycled, but grey and taupe pots, which are made from carbon-free polypropylene, can.

Seed tray
A seed tray made from fairtrade, natural rubber is essential for sowing seeds and growing plants on. Thick and flexible, yet easy to get the plants out of, it will last for years to come. I like trays with cells measuring 3 x 3 x 4cm (1¼ x 1¼ x 1½in).

Seeds or plants?

You have two options when acquiring the plants you need: growing them from seed or buying them as young plants in pots.

Growing from seed

- Sowing seed from scratch is enjoyable, as it is rewarding to see a fuzz of green emerge from something that looked like dust. Nurturing plants from the start of life is also a sure-fire way of increasing your knowledge of how plants grow, so you're better placed to respond to their needs later.

- In comparison to the cost of buying plants, growing from seed is very affordable. It offers the widest possible choice of varieties and in a much more nuanced range of colours. This is particularly true of annual plants, which are so inexpensive to buy as seeds, easy to germinate and fast to grow that they are almost never worth buying as plants.

- Growing plants from seed also has excellent environmental credentials, especially if you reuse or repurpose existing seed trays or pots. Plants from a nursery or garden centre tend to come in pots – albeit ones you can recycle – and are often grown in compost that includes peat.

- The amount of space you have is an important consideration, however. Not only does growing from seed require seed trays, pots, horticultural grit and compost, but you will also need somewhere to store these items when not in use. More important, perhaps, is the space required for newly germinated seedlings, which will need protection, as they are vulnerable to the weather and pests like slugs until they are much bigger. Keep the seedlings on a sunny, good-sized windowsill or in a covered area outside that receives plenty of light.

Buying plants

- Visiting a nursery, garden centre or garden superstore will allow you to see the plants you're planning to buy as well as stand them in a trolley to assess how they look together before deciding how well a scheme will work. This is invaluable at the early stages of putting plants together and will inevitably spark more ideas for potential plant combinations.

- Whereas timing is critical to seed sowing, plants have a fairly long shelf life and so purchasing plants in pots is a good alternative if you have missed the seed-sowing window.

- Most perennials need to grow for two or more years before they are big enough to flower, and buying a young plant leapfrogs this stage. It is ready to go straight into the garden.

- It can be difficult to rein in the number of plants when you're sowing enthusiastically at the start of spring, potentially wasting seeds, compost and pots. Buying the exact number of plants you need is more efficient.

Buying plants

New planting can look a bit patchy to begin with and so the temptation is to cram plants in, but it is important to keep the eventual width and height the plants will reach in mind. Contemporary designers often repeat the same plants throughout a space. This simplifies the design and fosters a sense of cohesion, so the overall look is unified.

To work out how many of each plant you will need, use a long tape measure to work out the length and width of your border and calculate the size of your planting area in square metres (or feet). You can then calculate the number of plants you will need to fill the space. As a guide, aim for three to five plants per square metre (10 square feet).

Sourcing plants, bulbs and seeds

Buying plants in person at the local garden centre, DIY superstore or flower market is a good option if you want to plant your garden on occasional days when you have a few hours to spare. This has the added benefit of allowing you to see the plants you are planning to buy, to check them over and, perhaps, even hone your choices.

The drawback of going out with a list and a shopping bag is that the variety of plants on offer is likely to be quite limited, which can be frustrating if are looking for specific plants. Garden centres typically only offer plants when they are at the peak of flowering, which, if you have planned your garden, isn't necessarily when you want to buy them.

Plants typically arrive in packaging that can easily be recycled. You don't need to plant them outside immediately but remove them from their packaging as soon as possible and water the compost thoroughly. Stand the pots outside, somewhere sheltered, and make sure the compost is kept damp.

If you do shop in person, look for plants with strong, healthy, green leaves growing in pots of just-damp compost. Always buy the smallest size you can, as a small plant in a small pot is less expensive and, more importantly, will adapt and settle more quickly in its new location, saving you time and effort on watering during the early stages of its life.

Before you buy your plants, tap each one out of its pot and examine the roots – what is happening inside the pot is much more important than what is happening above it. A few circling roots inside the pot and some new young roots poking out of the holes in the base are good signs, but the plant's roots shouldn't completely fill the pot, with little visible compost. At the same time, the compost shouldn't fall away completely when you remove the plant from its container, as this indicates that it has only just been repotted.

Many nurseries offer an online/mail-order service. Online suppliers are subject to reviews and you can expect to receive a healthy, well-packaged plant, sent out at the right time of year, to plant in your own garden. The online ordering process is swift and easy – you can search for the exact plant you want - and it is lovely to unwrap and open a box of plants that has been delivered safely to your door.

In common with plants, a range of seeds and bulbs are also available from garden centres and DIY superstores. However, you'll find a much wider choice of cultivars from online seed and bulb suppliers. In the UK, the peak time for ordering seeds is early spring, while spring-flowering bulbs, such as daffodils and tulips, are available to order in late summer and early autumn.

Botanical and common names

Many plants share the same common name, but a botanical name is unique to each plant. A plant's botanical name is usually made up of two or three words.

The first is the genus name, which is shared by many plants with the same characteristics – this is written in Latin and given in italics. The genus *Tulipa*, for example, is used to describe all the tulips in existence, so the botanical name of every tulip starts with the word '*Tulipa*'.

The second word in the botanical name, if there is one, is the species name. This describes a subgroup within the genus and is also italicized. An example would be *Cynara cardunculus*.

The third name, which is in roman print in inverted commas, is the cultivar name. A cultivar name denotes a plant that has been selected by a person as something special and grown to sell – for instance, *Tulipa* 'Spring Green'. This name was chosen by the person who bred the plant and often includes information about what makes it special, perhaps its colour or where it was originally bred – for example, *Nepeta racemosa* 'Walker's Low'.

Using a plant's botanical name is the only way to be sure the plant you are referring to, or searching for, is the one that you intend.

Some plants have the letters AGM (Award of Garden Merit) written after their name, which you will see on the plant label or when you search for them online. This means that the plant has been trialled by the Royal Horticultural Society (RHS) in the UK and been found to be the best of its type. Plants that are awarded AGM status have been judged as 'excellent for garden use', based on criteria such as availability, longevity and resilience to pests.

Dark plum-purple *Salvia* 'Nachtvlinder' (sage) and the two-tone pink *S.* 'Dyson's Joy'

How to grow plants from seed

A flat, even surface is essential for seed sowing, pricking out and potting on young plants. I use a homemade potting tray, which I made from a piece of plywood, measuring about 60 x 60cm (2 x 2ft), by fixing three lengths of wood to three edges to keep the compost in place. A piece of wood fixed under the front edge anchors the potting tray to the table and stops it sliding about. It's portable, lightweight and easy to store once seed sowing is over for the year. A kitchen tabletop would work just as well but, as I like to sow seeds little and often as time allows, it saves constantly having to get equipment out and tidy it away.

Spring is peak seed-sowing time. Growing plants from seed is as straightforward as putting a few seeds in a pot of compost and waiting for them to grow. It is the most sustainable way of gardening, using less fuel in comparison to the cost of transporting a plant, less compost and water, and fewer new plastic pots.

As a rule of thumb, sow small seeds earlier in the year than bigger seeds that have more reserves to get them up to the soil surface.

1

Use a gritty, peat-free compost – sharp drainage will encourage the emergent seedlings to extend their roots in a hunt for moisture, which will stand them in good stead later in life. Peat-free seed compost often contains bits of bark or bracken, so pick out any big lumps.

2

Fill a seed tray with seed compost, leaving a gap at the top of each cell for watering. Tap the tray on a flat surface to settle the compost and remove air pockets. This will also stop the compost sinking too much when you first water and provides a level surface for sowing.

3

Water the seed tray thoroughly, letting the water percolate through the compost.

COMPOST for SEEDS

4

Big seeds are best sown in twos, so you can remove the weakest seedling if both germinate. Sow small seeds in scant pinches – no more than four or five seeds per cell.

5

Place big seeds on the compost surface and use your finger to push them 2.5cm (1in) deep, letting the compost bury them. Sow smaller seeds on the compost surface.

6

Label the seed tray. When the seedlings have their first true leaves – rather than the cotyledons or 'seed leaves' – prick them out and transfer them to individual pots.

7

Using a pencil, gently lift one seedling out, holding it by a leaf and supporting the weight of its roots to avoid damaging the stem, which is fragile and liable to snap.

8

Plant the seedling in a prepared pot of compost at the same depth as in the seed tray. Use fingers to tuck compost around it and gently water using a rose attachment.

9

Grow the plant on somewhere with good light levels, which is crucial at this stage. Move it outside when roots begin to emerge from the pot base and there is growth at the tips.

How to arrange plants

How plants are arranged in relation to one another is a key part of any design. The aim is to space plants so they eventually cover the soil completely, with no bare earth visible between them, while giving each plant its own space. A healthy plant resilient to attack from pests and diseases is one that has room to grow without too much competition.

Keeping the plants in their pots to begin with, work out where you want them to go first. Choose one plant and work up a composition around it, aiming for a balance of heights and shapes. Tall plants such as thalictrum and veronicastrum are useful for creating rhythm, as the eye skips from one to another. Plants with flowers that appear to hover, like *Orlaya grandiflora* (white laceflower), also need to be placed carefully, as the empty space around them is as important as the space they take up. Use low-growing plants like thyme to keep air between taller plants, so that light can fall through, almost to ground level in places. After you have set out the plants, go away and come back later to look at the design with a fresh perspective and make any adjustments before planting up.

Pink is the leitmotif in this trio, which includes liquorice, plum, pink and lilac. The warm pink of the petals of *Papaver somniferum* (opium poppy) are well matched by the lilac umbels of *Tulbaghia violacea* (society garlic) and is repeated in a darker tone in the ruby foliage of *Atriplex hortensis* var. *rubra* (red orach). The poppy's chunky foliage also adds weight, anchoring what is otherwise a light and ethereal palette.

How to plant

Small plants in small pots are the choice of the sustainable gardener. Avoid planting on soaking wet or frosty days when the soil is easily damaged. The best time to plant is when rain is forecast. All plants grown in pots can be planted in the same way.

Start with perennials. Next, plant annuals and biennials between them and, lastly, add bulbs as a final layer.

1

Soak the new plant in its nursery pot using a watering can and leave to stand for a few minutes.

2

Using a trowel, dig a hole for the plant that is a little deeper and wider than the pot.

3

Take the plant out of its pot, giving the top of the pot a tap to release it if it doesn't come out easily. Using your fingertips, loosen some of the roots, especially if they have started to circle around inside the pot.

4

Plant your new plant at the same depth as it was in its pot, push back the soil around it and carefully firm it in with your hands. Don't push the soil down too firmly to avoid squashing the air out of it.

5

Water the soil around the plant thoroughly to settle it around the roots, aiming the water at the soil and not the foliage. Continue watering every one to two days until new green shoots appear.

How to plant bulbs

Bulbs that flower in spring, such as alliums, narcissi and tulips, need to be planted in autumn. This is because bulbs benefit from a cold snap while they are underground.

Bulbs that flower in summer, such as gladioli and dahlias, should be planted in late spring, after the risk of frost is over. Unlike young plants in small pots, the timing of the planting of a bulb is critical to its success.

1

Plant bulbs with their pointy ends facing upwards. Imagine the bulbs in flower and aim to keep like colours with like, as they would appear in nature, rather than mixing up the different colours.

2

Arrange the bulbs, pointy end up, on the surface of the soil. Next, use a trowel to dig a hole that is twice as deep as the height of the bulb, then drop it in.

3

Cover the bulb with soil and firm in carefully.

This pretty palette uses different colours in a common, bright hue. The purple flowers of *Allium hollandicum* 'Purple Sensation' (Dutch garlic) are picked up by the dark, tuft-like flowers of *Molinia caerulea* subsp. *caerulea* 'Poul Petersen' (purple moor-grass). Along with *Geum* 'Totally Tangerine' (avens) and *Papaver dubium* subsp. *lecoqii* 'Albiflorum' (Beth's poppy), their flowers appear to hover, allowing light to filter between them and highlighting the vibrancy of their colours.

Early spring	*Mid-spring*	*Late spring*	*Early summer*	*Mid-summer*
March	**April**	**May**	**June**	**July**
Sow the seeds of hardy annuals, such as poppies and *Cerinthe* indoors.	Prick out the seedlings of annuals, transplanting them into individual pots and moving them outside. Plant dahlia tubers and gladioli corms in pots and keep them protected from frost indoors. When the first of their green shoots push up, start watering them. Begin planting perennials like geums and *Hakonechloa* outside.	Continue planting perennials outside. Plan and plant up containers.	Sow the seeds of biennials such as *Verbascum.* Water containers regularly, soaking the compost thoroughly. Continue planting perennials outside. Continue planting containers, including those with plants that are vulnerable to frost, such as dahlias.	Water containers regularly – this may be as frequently as every day in warm weather. Continue to plant perennials outside.

Year-round planner

Late summer

August

Continue to water containers regularly.

Remove spent flowers (known as deadheading) to encourage further blooms.

Continue to plant perennials outside.

Early autumn

September

You can also sow the seeds of annuals this month for bigger plants that flower earlier next year.

Continue to plant perennials outside.

Plant biennials sown from seed outside, to flower next spring.

Mid-autumn

October

Order and plant spring-flowering bulbs such as daffodils and tulips.

Plant bulbs in containers.

Late autumn

November

Order summer-flowering bulbs, corms and tubers, such as gladioli and dahlias.

Late winter

February

Buy or order seeds online.

	January	February	March	April	May	June	July	August	September	October	November	December
Achillea 'Terracotta'						F	F	F				
Allium					F	F/S	F/S	F/S	S			
Anemone Wild Swan ('Macane001')					F	F	F	F	F	F/S	F/S	S
Asplenium scolopendrium	L	L	L	L	L	L	L	L	L	L	L	L
Astrantia major					F	F	F	F				
Briza media					F	F	F	F	S	S		
Catananche caerulea						F	F	F	F			
Cerinthe major 'Purpurascens'					F	F	F	F	F			
Cynara cardunculus						F	F	F	F			
Dahlia							F	F	F	F	F	
Dianthus carthusianorum							F	F	F			
Digitalis parviflora					F	F	F					
Dryopteris wallichiana	L	L	L	L	L	L	L	L	L	L	L	L
Eschscholzia californica 'Ivory Castle'						F	F	F				
Euphorbia seguieriana subsp. niciciana					F	F	F	F	F			
Geranium Rozanne ('Gerwat')					F	F	F	F	F	F		
Geum 'Lemon Drops'					F	F	F					
Gladiolus papilio							F	F				
Hakonechloa macra			S/L	S/L	S/L	F/L	F/L	S/L	S/L	S/L	S/L	S/L
Linaria maroccana 'Licilia Violet'						F	F	F	F	F		

Seasons of interest

	January	February	March	April	May	June	July	August	September	October	November	December
Melica altissima 'Alba'				**F**	**F**	**F**						
Narcissus			**F**	**F**								
Nepeta racemosa 'Walker's Low'						**F**	**F**	**F**	**F**			
Orlaya grandiflora					**F**	**F**	**F**	**F**				
Papaver (annual poppies)	**S**	**S**			**F**	**F/S**	**F/S**	**F/S**	**S**	**S**	**S**	**S**
Papaver (perennial poppies)						**F**	**F**	**F**	**S**	**S**	**S**	**S**
Pulsatilla vulgaris				**F**	**F**	**S**	**S**	**S**	**S**	**S**	**S**	
Rosa x *odorata* 'Mutabilis'					**F**	**F**	**F**	**F**	**F**	**F**	**F**	
Salvia 'Nachtvlinder'					**F**	**F**	**F**	**F**	**F**	**F**	**F**	
Salvia nemorosa 'Caradonna'						**F**	**F**	**F**	**F**	**F**		
Salvia officinalis 'Purpurascens'	**L**	**L**	**L**	**L**	**L/F**	**L/F**	**L/F**	**L**	**L**	**L**	**L**	**L**
Salvia rosmarinus	**L**	**L**	**L**	**L/F**	**L/F**	**L/F**	**L/F**	**L/F**	**L**	**L**	**L**	**L**
Sanguisorba officinalis 'Arnhem'						**F**	**F**	**F**				
Symphyotrichum 'Little Carlow'								**F**	**F**	**F**		
Thalictrum 'Elin'						**F**	**F**	**F**				
Thymus 'Fragrantissimus'	**L**	**L**	**L**	**L**	**L**	**L/F**	**L/F**	**L/F**	**L**	**L**	**L**	**L**
Tulbaghia violacea						**F**	**F**	**F**	**F**	**F**	**F**	
Tulipa				**F**	**F**							
Verbascum bombyciferum 'Polarsommer'					**F**	**F**	**S**	**S**	**S**	**S**	**S**	**S**
Verbena officinalis 'Bampton'						**F**	**F**	**F**	**F**			

F = Flowers
L = Foliage
S = Seedheads/Seedpods

Recommended resources

Tools

Burgon & Ball
Well-made gardening tools with wooden handles. Online and widely available in UK (EU and USA) in shops and garden centres.

burgonandball.com

Implementations
Copper gardening tools designed and built to last a lifetime.

implementations.co.uk

Niwaki
Well-made gardening tools and kit, as well as the essentials needed to keep tools in good order, such as sharpening stones. Niwaki also offer a mail-order tool-sharpening service.

niwaki.com

Seeds, plants and bulbs

Beth Chatto
Offer a wide selection of perennial plants and bulbs for delivery UK-wide. You can also visit the nursery to choose and collect plants.
Elmstead Market,
Colchester, Essex CO7 7DB

bethchatto.co.uk

Chiltern Seeds
An online seed supplier, offering an extensive range of interesting flower seeds. All seeds are supplied in glassine and paper envelopes and with detailed growing instructions.

chilternseeds.co.uk

Crocus
Crocus are Britain's largest online garden, plant and seed supplier and the choice of many garden designers. Over 4,000 different plants and varieties of seed are on offer, delivered in 100 per cent recyclable packaging.

crocus.co.uk

Farmer Gracy
This online supplier offers a well-chosen selection of bulbs, including for containers and shade, and those that are of benefit to pollinators.

farmergracy.co.uk

Organic Bulbs
An ecologically friendly bulb nursery offering bulbs that are useful for pollinators. All bulbs sold are chemical-free and British-grown.

organicbulbs.com

Sarah Raven
Trialling plants and seeds in her garden in Sussex, Sarah Raven finds the most covetable and the best, which she offers for sale online.

sarahraven.com

Special Plants
Offer an interesting selection of plants and seeds, including more unusual seeds. Some of the seeds on offer are best sown fresh and these are sent out at the right time of year for sowing. The nursery, in the southwest of the UK, is worth a special trip.

Greenways Lane, Cold Ashton,
Chippenham, Wiltshire SN14 8L

specialplants.net

Furniture

Fermob
Stylish and durable outdoor furniture and accessories.

fermob.com

Garden Trading
A selection of well-designed and contemporary garden staples, including furniture and outdoor lighting

gardentrading.co.uk

HAY
Cool, functional garden furniture, including the popular Palissade range. Made from weatherproof, powder-coated steel, in five colours, it is durable enough to be left outdoors all year.

hay.com

IKEA
Affordable and contemporary garden furniture suited to small outdoor spaces and designed to pack away easily where storage is limited.

ikea.com

Paint

Farrow & Ball
A range of low-VOC, water-based exterior paints in traditional and contemporary colours.

farrow-ball.com

Mylands x Jinny Blom
A palette of 12 low-VOC, water-based exterior paints in shades inspired by the natural landscape.

mylands.com

Tiles

Bert & May
Traditionally manufactured exterior tiles in various colours and shapes, as well as designs that are more graphic.

bertandmay.com

Featured designers

Alice Ferguson Garden Design
An independent design practice with an emphasis on well-thought-out planting designs. Bristol, UK

alicefergusongardendesign.co.uk

Arthur Parkinson
Garden writer, photographer and illustrator of chickens. Known for a love of bold colours and bees. Nottingham, UK

@arthurparkinson_

Artisan Landscapes
An award-winning garden and landscape design practice specializing in expertly crafted spaces. Bristol, UK

artisanlandscapes.co.uk

Colin Stewart
Gardener and artist. London, UK.

@colindavidstewart

Conrad Batten
Creates contemporary and sustainable garden designs with a focus on natural beauty. Totnes, UK

conradbatten.com

Ed O'Brien
Garden designer specializing in naturalistic gardens informed by climate and site. Bristol, UK

edobrien.co.uk

Garden Club London
London-based design studio specializing in contemporary designs for urban spaces, including roof gardens. London, UK

gardenclublondon.co.uk

Marc O'Neill
Planting consultant and designer, making gardens in the UK and Ireland. London, UK

@marcfinds

Matt Evans Landscapes
Chartered landscape architect and garden designer. Bath, UK.

mattevanslandscapes.com

Miria Harris
Colour is at the heart of this creative, modern studio. London, UK

miriaharris.com

Sarah Price Landscapes
Multi-award-winning garden designer recognized for her nature-inspired and painterly approach. Monmouthshire, UK

sarahpricelandscapes.com

Thanks to:

The Exchange
A community-owned garden in Greenwich, London, designed by Sarah Price with head gardener Colin Stewart.
The Exchange, The Old Library,

Walnut Tree Road,
Erith DA8 1RA

theexchangeerith.com

Index

Italic page numbers indicate illustrations

First published in
Great Britain in 2025 by
Mitchell Beazley, an imprint of
Octopus Publishing Group Ltd
Carmelite House
50 Victoria Embankment
London EC4Y 0DZ
www.octopusbooks.co.uk

An Hachette UK Company
www.hachette.co.uk

The authorized representative in the EEA is Hachette Ireland, 8 Castlecourt Centre, Dublin 15, D15 XTP3, Ireland (email: info@hbgi.ie)

Distributed in the US by
Hachette Book Group
1290 Avenue of the Americas,
4th and 5th Floors
New York, NY 10104

Distributed in Canada by
Canadian Manda Group
664 Annette St., Toronto,
Ontario, Canada M6S 2C8

ISBN 978 1 78472 934 9

Printed and bound in China.

10 9 8 7 6 5 4 3 2 1

Publishing Director:
Alison Starling
Creative Director:
Jonathan Christie
Photographer:
Jason Ingram
Book Designer: Untitled
Senior Managing Editor:
Sybella Stephens
Copy Editor: Caroline West
Senior Production Manager:
Katherine Hockley

Author's acknowledgements
Thank you to Alison Starling, Jonathan Christie, David Hawkins, Sybella Stephens, Caroline West and Katherine Hockley, the dream team at Octopus.

To Jason Ingram, my favourite photographer.

To The Exchange, Erith, Sarah Price, Colin Stewart, Miria Harris, Matt Evans, Conrad Batten, Tony Woods, Arthur Parkinson, Ed O'Brien, Marc O'Neill, Eleanor Pritchard, Will Cooke, BBC *Gardeners' World* magazine.

To Anne, Bill and Victoria.